VOCABULARY
BUILDER

SPANISH

Mastering the Most Common
Spanish Words and Phrases

by
Rosalía de Rösler

BARRON'S

This symbol ➤ marks practical tips that make learning fast and easy.

All inquiries should be addressed to:
Barron's Educational Series, Inc.
250 Wireless Boulevard
Hauppauge, NY 11788
http://www.barronseduc.com

International Standard Book Number 0-7641-1824-2

Library of Congress Catalog Card Number 2001086135

Printed in the United States of America
9 8 7 6 5 4 3 2

Table of Contents

Chapter 1

Expand Your Vocabulary
Amplíe su vocabulario 5
1.1 How to Use This Book . . . 6
1.2 Word Classes 6
1.3 How to Use a Dictionary . . 7
1.4 Words and Their
Definitions 8
1.5 Idiomatic Expressions in
Spanish 9
1.6 Word Families 9
1.7 Opposites 10
1.8 Sentences and Pictures . . . 11
1.9 Reading Comprehension . . 12
1.10 Vocabulary Chart 14

Chapter 2

Word Groups
Grupos de palabras 15
2.1 Which Word Goes with
Which Topic? 16
2.2 Which Words Are Left? . . . 17
2.3 Days of the Week and Parts
of the Day 18
2.4 Months and Seasons 19
2.5 The Date 19
2.6 Numbers 20
2.7 Wishes and
Congratulations 21
2.8 Stating Your Opinion 21
2.9 Expressing Disappointment,
Pleasure, and Displeasure . . 22
2.10 Verbs of Motion 22

Chapter 3

Topics
Temas 23
3.1 Personal Data 24
3.2 Nationalities 25
3.3 Occupations 26

3.4 Family and Relationships . . 27
3.5 Describing People 28
3.6 Feelings 29
3.7 House 30
3.8 Leisure Activities 32
3.9 Sports 33
3.10 Cities, Villages, and
Landscapes 34
3.11 In Town 35
3.12 Means of Transportation . . 36
3.13 Modern Means of
Communication 37
3.14 Stores 38
3.15 Restaurant and Bar 39
3.16 Foods 40
3.17 Vacation 42
3.18 Money 43
3.19 Weather 44
3.20 Time 45

Chapter 4

Word Formation
Formación de palabras 46
4.1 Adverb Formation 47
4.2 Prefixes 48
4.3 Noun and Adjective 48
4.4 Verb and Noun 49
4.5 Noun Formation 50

Chapter 5

Pronunciation and Spelling
Pronunciación y ortografía 51
5.1 Pronunciation 52
5.2 Stress 53
5.3 Written Accent 53

Chapter 6

Word Combinations
Combinaciones de palabras 54
6.1 Verbs with Different
Meanings 55
6.2 Useful Verbs 56
6.3 Verbs 57
6.4 Verbs + Nouns, Adjectives,
and Adverbs 58
6.5 *Qué* + Noun, Adjective, and
Adverb 59

Chapter 7

Situations
Situaciones 60
7.1 Saying Hello and
Good-bye 61
7.2 Arranging to Meet 62
7.3 On the Telephone 63
7.4 At a Party 64
7.5 At the Train Station and at
the Airport 65
7.6 Going Shopping 66
7.7 At the Market 67
7.8 Ordering a Meal 68
7.9 Asking for Directions 69
7.10 Going on Vacation 70
7.11 At the Hotel 71
7.12 A Tourist in Latin
America 72
7.13 Emergencies 73
7.14 Renting an Apartment . . . 74
7.15 At the Doctor's Office 75
7.16 Looking for a Job 76

Chapter 8

Grammar
Gramática 78
8.1 The Noun and Its
Companions 79
8.2 Noun and Adjective 80
8.3 *Muy, mucho,* and *poco* . . . 81
8.4 Adjective and Adverb . . . 82

8.5 Regular Verbs 83
8.6 Irregular Verbs 84
8.7 *Hay, estar,* and *ser* 86
8.8 The Near Future 87
8.9 The Progressive Form . . . 88
8.10 Preterit or Imperfect 89
8.11 *Poder* and *saber* 90
8.12 Possessive Adjectives . . . 90
8.13 Interrogative Words 91
8.14 The Prepositions *a, para, por,
en, de* 92
8.15 Indications of Place 93
8.16 Negation 94
8.17 Comparative and
Superlative 95

Chapter 9

Word Games
Juegos de palabras 96
9.1 Word Puzzle 97
9.2 My Aunt from Zaragoza . . 98
9.3 Riddles 99

Test 1 100
Test 2 101
Test 3 102
Test 4 103
Test 5 104

Answers 105

Glossary 109

Chapter 1

Amplíe su vocabulario
Expand Your Vocabulary

1. Set up a card index of words.

Using an index file makes it easy to memorize words, and it is also a good way to learn correct spelling. On one side of the index card, write the Spanish word, and under it write a sentence containing the word. On the back of the card, note the English translation of the word you want to memorize.

2. Write, speak, and listen to Spanish.

Because writing, speaking, reading, and listening involve several sense organs in the language-acquisition process, you can learn words and their meaning more easily.

3. Pay attention to grammatical constructions.

When you're learning new words, memorize the gender of nouns or irregular forms of verbs at the same time.

4. Read material in Spanish.

Whenever you can, read material in Spanish. You'll be surprised how many opportunities there will be: For example, when shopping, you can easily memorize the Spanish names of a few products, since product names and descriptions increasingly are provided in Spanish as well. Similarly, you can quickly learn a few food names when you eat in a Spanish or Latin American restaurant and are given a menu in two languages. Alternatively, you can page through a Spanish-language newspaper or magazine and read a few short articles or ads.

5. Often there's not enough time to study vocabulary.

You'll be amazed to see how quickly you progress if you use every possible opportunity to enlarge your vocabulary: at home, on the bus, on the subway, at the swimming pool, and so forth.

1.1 Cómo utilizar este libro
How to Use This Book

1. First, work your way through the entire first chapter.

2. Next, look at the other chapters and choose the exercises you want to work on. You can determine the sequence yourself. Start with the chapters and exercises that deal with topics that interest you or areas that you want to focus on. That way you will have a chance to pinpoint your own areas of difficulty in Spanish, and then to eliminate them.

3. At the end of the book are five tests that you can use to measure your progress.

4. While you work with this book, keep a dictionary nearby as well, so that you can get additional information about the spelling, pronunciation, or meaning of words.

5. A vocabulary notebook is an indispensable study aid. In it, you can enter words that you have trouble memorizing or words that you find difficult.

1.2 Clases de palabras
Word Classes

 The grammatical terms on the left are words that you will come across repeatedly when you learn a foreign language.

Match the words in boldface in the right-hand column with the terms on the left. Enter your answers in the boxes below the exercise. We've already supplied one answer for you.

1. Adjetivo	a.	**Ella** está en Madrid.
2. Adverbio	b.	María vive en el **primer** piso.
3. Artículo	c.	**Hablar** español es importante.
4. Sustantivo	d.	Argentina es un país **muy** grande.
5. Preposición	e.	Tenemos un **coche** azul.
6. Numerales	f.	La casa es **grande**.
7. Pronombre personal	g.	**El** chico está enfermo.
8. Verbo	h.	José compra frutas **y** patatas.
9. Conjunción	i.	María va **en** tren **a** Barcelona.

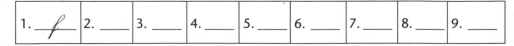

| 1. _f_ | 2. ___ | 3. ___ | 4. ___ | 5. ___ | 6. ___ | 7. ___ | 8. ___ | 9. ___ |

1.3 Cómo utilizar el diccionario
How to Use a Dictionary

A word can have a variety of different meanings. Usually, dictionaries list several variants.

First, read through this dictionary entry for the word **hacer**. *Then it will be a snap for you to translate the Spanish sentences below into correct English.*

hacer [-'θer] *irr* **1.** *vt* to make; to do; *(crear)* to create; *(fabricar)* to manufacture; *(preparar)* to prepare; *(ejecutar)* to carry out; *(obligar)* to compel; **2.** *vi (parecer)* to appear, to seem; **3.** *vr:* *~se (transformarse)* to become; *(fabricarse)* to be made; *~se con algo* to provide oneself with s.th.; *~se a un lado* to step aside; *~se a la mar* to put to sea; *~se el sordo* to pretend to be deaf; *~se viejo* to grow old; *~ de* to act as; *~ las maletas* to pack one's bags; *~ una pregunta* to ask a question; *~ una visita* to pay a visit; *~ como que, ~ como si* to act as if; *~ bien/mal* to do the right/wrong thing; *~ de malo (TEAT)* to play the villain; *hace frío/calor* it is cold/hot; *hace dos años* two years ago; *hace poco* a short time ago; *¿qué ~?* what can we do?; *me hice un traje* I had a suit made for myself.

Source: PONS Standardwörterbuch [Standard Dictionary], Ernst Klett Verlag, Stuttgart

1. ¿Qué hacemos hoy? _____

2. Juan se ha hecho viejo. _____

3. Hoy hace mucho frío. _____

4. ¿Hacemos la comida juntos? _____

5. ¡Haz las maletas, por favor! _____

1.4 Palabras y sus definiciones
Words and Their Definitions

Being able to define words has many advantages.
For one thing, you can learn new words more easily if you also know their definitions. For another, you can speak about things, persons, or circumstances for which you don't have the right word readily available.

Moreover, it's not possible to find an English equivalent for every Spanish word. For many items and concepts specific to Spanish-speaking countries, there is no equivalent in another language. These words require definition and explanation. Here are some examples that you could find in a monolingual dictionary:

lavadora *f* máquina para lavar ropa

gazpacho *m* sopa fría de tomates, pepinos, pimientos, cebollas, sal, aceite, ajo y vinagre

Match the words in the box below with the following definitions.

el hotel	el turista	el palacio	la estación	la plaza
la familia	los habitantes	la paella	el invierno	la playa

1. El sitio donde llegan los trenes. _____

2. Personas que viven en un pueblo. _____

3. Está en la costa donde hay mucha arena. _____

4. Está en el centro de un pueblo. _____

5. El lugar donde se duerme en las vacaciones. _____

6. Cuando hace mucho frío y cae nieve. _____

7. Una casa muy grande donde viven los reyes. _____

8. Un plato que se hace con arroz. _____

9. El padre, la madre y los hijos. _____

10. Extranjero que visita un país. _____

1.5 Combinaciones típicas en español
Idiomatic Expressions in Spanish

Whenever you want to fix a word in your memory, it's a good idea to learn it in combination with other words.

Which words in the box below go with the following verbs?

de ~~casa~~	un paseo	hambre	al tenis
al cine	las camas	una cerveza	en casa

1. cambiar *de casa*
2. hacer _____
3. tomar _____
4. ir _____

5. tener _____
6. dar _____
7. quedarse _____
8. jugar _____

1.6 Familia de palabras
Word Families

When you find a word in the dictionary, try to derive other words from it, as in these examples:

interés　　　→　　　interesar　　　→　　　interesante

Complete the sentences by changing the words in the shaded box.

1. Es una película muy *interesante*	interesar
2. Mario _____ mucho.	trabajo
3. ¿Dónde se puede pedir _____?	informar
4. La leche es _____ para los niños.	necesitar
5. ¿Cuál es el _____ para el pueblo?	caminar
6. La _____ es a las ocho.	cenar
7. De Madrid a Berlín es un _____ largo.	viajar

1.7 **Contrarios**
Opposites

You can enlarge and practice your vocabulary by forming opposites.

In the blank below each picture, write a word opposite in meaning to the adjective or noun accompanying the picture.

largo   bajo   limpio   ligero   triste   malo
nuevo   viejo   correcto   grande   noche   calor

alegre   pequeño   antiguo   alto

1. *triste*   2. _____   3. _____   4. _____

corto   sucio   bueno   día

5. _____   6. _____   7. _____   8. _____

falso   pesado   joven   frío

9. _____   10. _____   11. _____   12. _____

1.8 Combinación de imágenes y frases

Sentences and Pictures

Some information can be conveyed more clearly, quickly, and lastingly through pictures. If you look at these pictures while studying the vocabulary, and then write the Spanish words and say them aloud simultaneously, you'll be learning on several "channels" at once.

Look at the pictures. Then read the following sentences. Next, write the appropriate sentences under each picture.

1. A mí me gusta viajar en tren.
2. ¡Qué calor hace aquí en el desierto!
3. Las ciudades grandes me parecen muy peligrosas.
4. Es un día de verano en la playa.
5. ¡Qué bonito atardecer y el sol entre los cactos!
6. El tren llega a las dos.
7. ¡Qué edificio más alto!
8. No quieren nadar porque el agua está fría.

Picture 1

Picture 2

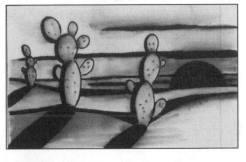

Picture 3

Picture 4

Comprensión de lectura

Reading Comprehension

Don't be afraid of unfamiliar reading material! Try to get the gist of the material, even though you don't know every word. Not all information is essential to an understanding of a text.

Read the passage and mark all the words and word combinations that are useful to you.

La bicicleta.

Don Pepe vive en un pueblo español cerca de la frontera francesa, en Cataluña. Su pueblo es muy pequeño; tiene unos tres mil habitantes y, como todos los pueblos españoles, tiene una plaza en el centro, con una fuente. Delante de la plaza, al lado de la farmacia, tiene don Pepe una tienda. Todos los días muy temprano, por las mañanas, sale de su casa y cruza la frontera. Unas horas más tarde regresa, en bicicletà, a su tienda. El guardia en la frontera piensa que don Pepe contrabandea algo, porque es muy raro que todos los días pase la frontera y al regresar no lleve nada.

Por eso, todos los días revisa el guardia a don Pepe, busca en su bolso, en los pantalones, en fin, busca por todas partes, sin encontrar nada. Siempre hace las mismas preguntas:

— "¿Trae Ud. cigarrillos, chocolates, bebidas alcohólicas?"

La respuesta es siempre la misma:

— "No, no traigo ni cigarrillos, ni chocolates, ni alcohol", — dice don Pepe y pasa por la frontera, sin problemas.

Así, todos los días, durante veinte años. Ahora tanto don Pepe como el guardia de la frontera están jubilados. Un día se encuentran los dos en el bar del pueblo.

— "Dígame, don Pepe, aquí en confianza, yo estoy seguro que usted ha contrabandeado algo durante veinte años, ahora me puede decir la verdad" —, le pregunta el guardia muy curioso a don Pepe.

Don Pepe, sonriendo, le dice:

— "Pues la verdad, sí he contrabandeado algo en los últimos veinte años, ¿sabe Ud. qué...?"

— "No" — le contesta el guardia, mirando a don Pepe directamente en los ojos.

— "Pues, ¡bicicletas!" — le responde don Pepe irónico.

Drill 1

Read the passage again and indicate whether the statements below are true or false.

	sí	no
1. Don Pepe tiene una tienda delante de la farmacia.		
2. El guardia desea saber si don Pepe lleva algo.		
3. Don Pepe regresa por las tardes, en coche.		
4. El guardia y don Pepe se encuentran en el bar los fines de semana.		
5. Después de veinte años, el guardia sabe la verdad.		
6. Don Pepe contrabandea cigarrillos.		

Drill 2

Look at the word combinations in the passage. Fill in the missing words.

1. Adjectives + Nouns

a. un pueblo *español*

b. la frontera _____

c. las bebidas _____

d. el guardia _____

2. Verbs + Prepositions

a. vivir _____ un pueblo

b. salir _____ su casa

c. regresar _____ la tienda

d. pasar _____ la frontera

e. buscar _____ su bolso

f. preguntar _____ don Pepe

3. Indications of Time

a. _____ los días

b. muy _____ por las mañanas

c. unas horas más _____

d. _____ veinte años

e. _____ día se encuentran

f. en los _____ veinte años

4. Nouns + Nouns

a. los habitantes del _____

b. la plaza del _____

c. la bicicleta de _____

d. la fuente de _____

e. la tienda de _____

f. el bar del _____

g. el guardia de la _____

1.10 Asociación de tópicos
Vocabulary Chart

A good way to associate words with a certain topic is to create a vocabulary chart like the one shown here. It is intended to help you organize new vocabulary according to subject. It also is a good way to drill vocabulary.

Using the following words, fill in the blanks in the chart.

restaurante	tren	habitación	hotel
pasaporte	gafas de sol	teatro	cine
cheque de viaje	coche	traje de baño	tienda

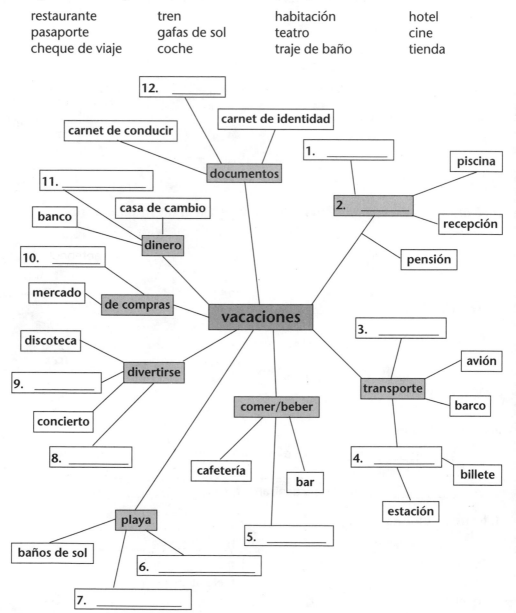

Chapter 2

Grupos de palabras
Word Groups

1. Classification of concepts.

When you're compiling your personal lexicon, try to classify the words according to subject or in groups. You can learn new terms more easily and efficiently if they are clearly arranged by subject matter. Your fund of words related to specific topics will increase as well.

For example:

—words for professions and occupations
—words for foods.

2. Create word groupings in your vocabulary notebook.

Write each new word that you want to learn in your vocabulary notebook, and enter it under whatever general heading you have chosen.

3. Expand your vocabulary of words dealing with specific topics.

In your vocabulary notebook, write down all the words you can think of dealing with a certain general topic. Then expand your vocabulary by using a dictionary to look up words that interest you and adding them to your notebook.

2.1 ¿A qué tema corresponde qué palabra?
Which Word Goes with Which Topic?

 Make a list of all the words that you know concerning a certain topic. Never learn new words in isolation; always learn them in connection with other words.

Arrange the following nouns under the correct headings. Write each word in the appropriate column.

manzana	médico	jugar	silla	coche	carne
avión	arte	música	leer	arroz	mecánico
excursión	sopa	cama	pescado	radio	autobús
nevera	verdura	barco	mesa	armario	profesor
toros	tren	conductor	taxi	policía	campesino

1. Alimentos	2. Oficios	3. Transporte
manzana		

4. Objetos caseros	5. Tiempo libre

16

¿Qué palabras sobran?
Which Words Are Left?

In each line, cross out the word that doesn't belong.

1. frío	calor	viento	lluvia	~~día~~
2. estrella	río	montaña	isla	lago
3. brazo	ojo	vista	estómago	pierna
4. café	té	leche	hielo	cerveza
5. cuarto	calle	cocina	baño	lavabo
6. alto	moreno	chico	guapo	rubio
7. padre	hijo	marido	hermano	amigo
8. madre	periodista	peluquero	ingeniero	abogado
9. cuchillo	cama	tenedor	plato	cuchara
10. vivir	ir	estar	pasar	debajo
11. debajo de	encima de	al lado de	antes	delante de
12. supermercado	tienda	bar	librería	zapatería
13. saber	beber	comer	desayunar	cenar
14. pantalones	mesa	camisa	jersey	abrigo
15. vivo	soy	haces	tengo	voy
16. francés	italiano	suiza	alemán	inglés
17. pollo	sopa	tortilla	vaso	filete

2.3 Días de la semana y partes del día
Days of the Week and Parts of the Day

Parts of the day:

Until 12:00:	*por la mañana*
From 12:00 until 14:00:	*al mediodía*
From 14:00 until 19:00:	*por la tarde*
From 20:00 until 24:00:	*por la noche*

What is María doing this week? Write down what she is doing in the morning, at midday, in the afternoon, and in the evening.

	Lunes	Martes	Miércoles	Jueves	Viernes	Sábado	Domingo
9:00	*dentista*			*nadar*			
10:00		*Correos*					
13:00					*restaurante*		
15:00			*tenis*				
16:00	*gimnasia*			*compras*			*visita*
21:00		*cine*					
21:30						*discoteca*	

1. Dentista *el lunes por la mañana.*

2. Cine _____

3. Tenis _____

4. Visita _____

5. Gimnasia _____

6. Compras _____

7. Restaurante _____

8. Discoteca _____

9. Correos_____

10. Nadar _____

18

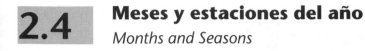

2.4 Meses y estaciones del año
Months and Seasons

Fill in the following months and seasons.

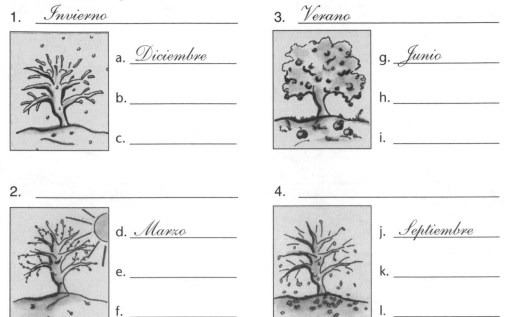

1. _Invierno_

   a. _Diciembre_

   b. _____

   c. _____

3. _Verano_

   g. _Junio_

   h. _____

   i. _____

2. _____

   d. _Marzo_

   e. _____

   f. _____

4. _____

   j. _Septiembre_

   k. _____

   l. _____

 Fecha
The Date

When did the following events take place?
Match the dates with the events, and write out the date in words, as shown in the example.

21.7.1969	2.9.1945	22.11.1963	6.8.1945
12.10.1492	3.10.1990	17.12.1830	

1. La muerte de Simón Bolívar   _el 17 de diciembre de 1830_

2. El descubrimiento de América _____

3. El primer hombre en la luna _____

4. La bomba atómica en Hiroshima _____

5. El final de la segunda guerra mundial _____

6. El asesinato del presidente Kennedy _____

7. La reunificación alemana _____

Don't forget that starting with the number 30, "*y*" always has to come between the tens and the units. All the hundreds (except 100) and the number 1 agree with the gender of the noun that follows.

Examples: *doscientas pesetas - trescientos marcos*
                 veintiún coches - veintiuna casas

Drill 1

Spell out the numbers.

Number	Thousands	Hundreds	Tens	Units
1. 1934	*mil*	*novecientos*	*treinta*	*y cuatro*
2. 3250				
3. 147				
4. 262				
5. 4585				
6. 421				
7. 2310				
8. 799				

Drill 2

Match the numbers with the words.

a. doscientas   b. trescientos   c. quinientas
d. veintitrés   e. diecinueve   f. mil novecientos

1. *(200)* _____ naranjas   4. *(19)* _____ niñas

2. *(23)* _____ años   5. *(1900)* _____ habitantes

3. *(500)* _____ pesetas   6. *(300)* _____ coches

2.7 Felicitaciones y buenos deseos
Wishes and Congratulations

Keep this in mind: After *"que"* to indicate wishing or wanting, the subjunctive is always used.

How do you express wishes and congratulations in Spanish? Match the expressions on the left with those on the right. Write the correct answers in the boxes.

1.	¡Felicidades!	a.	Merry Christmas!	1. *e*
2.	¡Que se mejore!	b.	Good-bye and good luck!	2. ___
3.	¡Buen provecho!	c.	Get well soon!	3. ___
4.	¡Feliz Navidad!	d.	Bon appétit!	4. ___
5.	¡Que lo pases bien!	e.	Congratulations!	5. ___

2.8 Expresar opiniones
Stating Your Opinion

You can express positive [☺] or negative [☹] opinions about various things or people. Try to write the following expressions in the columns where they belong. Of course, there are some expressions that are neither positive nor negative. Put them in this column: [😐].

1. Me parece demasiado feo.
2. ¡Es una buena idea!
3. ¡Qué guapo!
4. Tiene razón.
5. La blusa le va mal.
6. ¡Es fantástico cómo lo hace!
7. ¡Qué viaje tan aburrido!
8. ¡Conduce Ud. fatal!
9. Lo hago porque me gusta.
10. Es muy probable.
11. Creo que viene.
12. Hay que hacerlo enseguida.
13. Es indudable que es muy inteligente.
14. No me parece bien.
15. Comete Ud. un error.
16. ¡Qué tontería!

☺	☹	😐
¡Es una buena idea!		

2.9 Expresar desilusiones, gustos y desagrados

Expressing Disappointment, Pleasure, and Displeasure

Which statement (1–8) corresponds to the following situations (a–h)?

1. ¡Le hace mucha ilusión!
2. ¡Qué lástima!
3. Es insoportable.
4. He esperado otra cosa.
5. Estoy enfadadísimo.
6. Le tengo cariño.
7. ¡Qué sorpresa!
8. Es trágico, es terrible.

a. Ud. habla de una persona a la que quiere mucho.
b. Ud. recibe algo que no le gusta.
c. Un amigo no aprueba un examen.
d. Su amiga hace planes para su viaje.
e. De repente llega alguien a quien usted no espera.
f. Ud. se entera del accidente de alguien muy querido.
g. A Ud. le cuentan de alguien muy antipático.
h. Ud. ha peleado coléricamente con una persona.

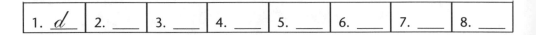

| 1. *d* | 2. ___ | 3. ___ | 4. ___ | 5. ___ | 6. ___ | 7. ___ | 8. ___ |

2.10 Verbos de movimientos

Verbs of Motion

 Verbs can be grouped according to various criteria. For example, you can learn the following groups of verbs in order to expand your vocabulary: action verbs, verbs of being, and verbs that show state of being. It's a good idea to learn verbs along with the prepositions that accompany them.

Use the following verbs to complete the sentences. The prepositions will help you.

ir   llegar   entrar   pasar   venir

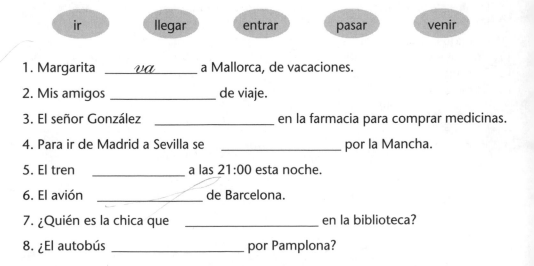

1. Margarita ___*va*___ a Mallorca, de vacaciones.

2. Mis amigos _____ de viaje.

3. El señor González _____ en la farmacia para comprar medicinas.

4. Para ir de Madrid a Sevilla se _____ por la Mancha.

5. El tren _____ a las 21:00 esta noche.

6. El avión _____ de Barcelona.

7. ¿Quién es la chica que _____ en la biblioteca?

8. ¿El autobús _____ por Pamplona?

Chapter 3

Temas
Topics

1. Arrange your words according to individual topics.

This chapter will help you arrange vocabulary words according to specific topics. If you file the words you collect under subject headings, you'll find it easier to learn new vocabulary.

2. Use pictures as a study aid.

Many words can be learned more quickly with the help of visual images. Try to describe postcards, catalogs, and pictures as a way of acquiring new words. Be bold; try putting together your own picture dictionary.

3. Make vocabulary charts.

Think about various words or idiomatic expressions that deal with the same subject, and put together a vocabulary chart.

3.1 Información personal
Personal Data

Drill 1

Match the questions in the left-hand column with the correct answers on the right.

1. ¿Es usted católico?
2. Me llamo María. ¿Y tú?
3. ¿De dónde eres?
4. ¿Eres ingeniero?
5. ¿Cuántos años tienes?
6. Soy de Perú. ¿Y tú también?

a. Tengo 32 años.
b. Sí, trabajo en una empresa de construcción.
c. No, soy protestante.
d. No, yo soy de Bolivia, soy boliviano.
e. Me llamo Marta.
f. Soy español, de Madrid.

1. _____	2. _____	3. _____	4. _____	5. _____	6. _____

Drill 2

Match the English sentences with their Spanish equivalents.

1. What is your name?
2. Where are you from?
3. Are you married?
4. Where do you live?
5. Do you have children?
6. What is your occupation?
7. I am single.

a. ¿Dónde vive usted?
b. ¿Tiene hijos?
c. ¿A qué te dedicas?
d. ¿Es usted casado?
e. Soy soltero.
f. ¿De dónde es usted?
g. ¿Cómo se llama usted?

1._____	2._____	3._____	4._____	5._____	6._____	7._____

3.2 Nacionalidades
Nationalities

Drill 1

Fill in the blanks with the missing words. Pay attention to feminine and masculine adjective endings.

País	Nacionalidad	
	Masculino	Femenino
1. Perú	peruano	_____
2. _____	español	española
3. Suiza	_____	suiza
4. Venezuela	venezolano	_____
5. Alemania	alemán	_____
6. _____	ecuatoriano	ecuatoriana
7. Austria	austríaco	_____
8. Inglaterra	inglés	_____

Drill 2

Fill in the blanks with the adjectives of nationality for the countries indicated.

1. El Renault es un coche *francés* .   Francia

2. Estos vinos son _____   Italia

3. El queso _____ es muy bueno.   Holanda

4. Las playas _____son hermosas.   España

5. Boris Becker es un famoso tenista _____   Alemania

6. El tango es un baile _____   Argentina

7. Gabriel García Márquez es un escritor _____   Colombia

3.3 Profesiones
Occupations

Drill 1

Complete the sentences with the nouns provided.

maestra estudiante hospital ingeniero azafata oficina camarero

1. Mario es médico, trabaja en un _____

2. María es _____ , trabaja en una escuela.

3. Un _____ trabaja en un restaurante.

4. Javier es _____ , estudia en la universidad.

5. Josefina es empleada, trabaja en una _____

6. Carlos es _____ , trabaja en una oficina de construcción.

7. Luisa es _____ , ella atiende a los pasajeros del avión.

Drill 2

Match the nouns denoting occupation with the appropriate pictures.

cocinero   secretaria   peluquera   mecánico   dentista   bombero

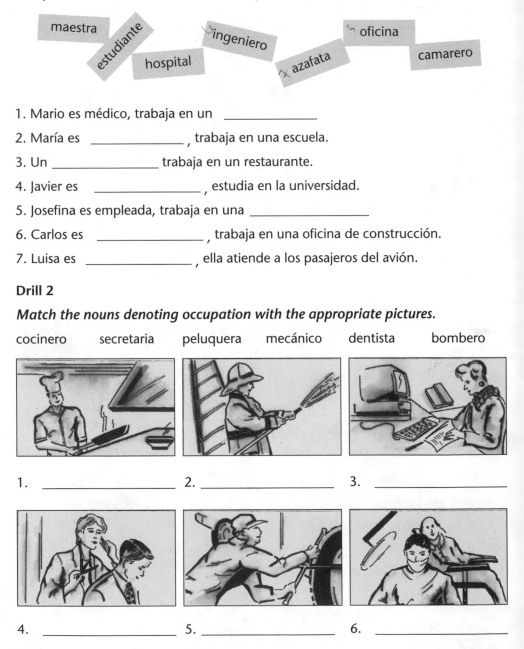

1. _____   2. _____   3. _____

4. _____   5. _____   6. _____

Familia y parientes
Family and Relatives

Read the passage, and then enter the appropriate names in the family tree.

Pedro tiene tres nietos: Isabel, Pedrito y Carlos. Los padres de Isabel y Carlos se llaman Iris y Jorge. Jorge es el yerno de Pedro y tiene además dos cuñados: Ernesto, que está casado con Miriam, y Gabriela que está soltera. La esposa de Pedro se llama Rosa. Ernesto y Miriam tienen un bebé: Pedrito.

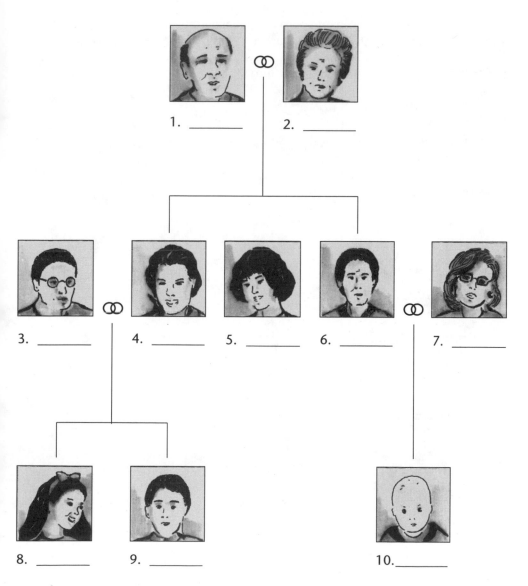

1. _____   2. _____

3. _____   4. _____   5. _____   6. _____   7. _____

8. _____   9. _____   10. _____

3.5 Describir personas
Describing People

Remember that *"ser"* is used to describe a state or condition that is lasting rather than accidental or occasional. *"Estar,"* on the other hand, is used to express conditions that are accidental or temporary, to show location or position, or to express evaluations or opinions.

Write the following descriptions under the appropriate pictures.

1. Mario es un poco calvo y hoy está muy triste.
2. Josefina es morena, lleva gafas y es muy simpática.
3. Mariana es rubia, muy elegante pero es un poco gorda.
4. Elsa y Eugenia son rubias, muy guapas y son también buenas amigas.
5. Juan es alto, moreno y siempre está bien vestido.
6. Gerardo es chistoso pero es feísimo y fuma mucho.

a. _____

_____

b. _____

_____

c. _____

_____

d. _____

_____

e. _____

_____

f. _____

_____

28

3.6 Sentimientos
Feelings

How do the people shown in these pictures feel?
Match the sentences with the drawings.

1. Gloria y Carmen tienen miedo.
2. Están felices.
3. El niño está muy triste.
4. Está enfadada con Ana.

5. Está furioso.
6. Están desilusionados.
7. Odia a su hermana.
8. Está muy preocupado.

a. _____

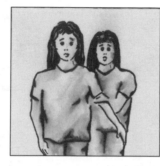

b. _____

c. _____

d. _____

e. _____

f. _____

g. _____

h. _____

3.7 La casa
House

Drill 1

Enter the correct terms into the boxes.

el jardín	la cocina	el lavabo	la ventana	el techo	la chimenea
el dormitorio	la sala de estar	la puerta	el garaje	el baño	

Drill 2

In which room would you put the following objects? Assign the objects below to the correct rooms.

la mesa   el armario   la almohada   la cama   el sofá   el sillón   el televisor
el horno   la cocina   la mesilla de noche   la nevera   las sillas   la lámpara de pie

El cuarto de estar:

1. _____

2. _____

3. _____

4. _____

La cocina:

1. _____

2. _____

3. _____

El dormitorio:

1. _____

2. _____

3. _____

4. _____

El comedor:

1. *la mesa* _____

2. _____

Using *"gustar,"* you can express preferences for something or someone.

Beatriz and Nelson are good friends, but they take part in different leisure activities. Look at the pictures, and then list their hobbies. Use the following terms.

hacer fotos	tocar la guitarra	coleccionar sellos	jugar a las cartas
escuchar música clásica	ver la televisión	leer novelas	escuchar música pop
hacer punto	leer tebeos	coser	hacer películas de vídeo

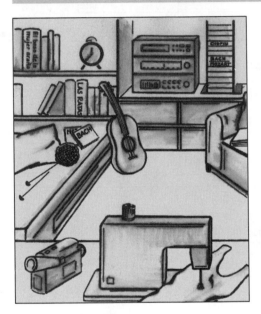 

1. A Beatriz le gusta: _____

_____

_____

2. A Nelson le gusta: _____

_____

_____

3.9 **Deportes**
Sports

Which sports are you familiar with? Match the following sports with the appropriate pictures.

jugar al fútbol	hacer ciclismo	hacer equitación
patinar sobre hielo	jugar al baloncesto	jugar al tenis
nadar	hacer la vela	esquiar
jugar al balonmano	hacer atletismo	jugar al golf

1. _____

2. _____

3. _____

4. _____

5. _____

6. _____

7. _____

8. _____

9. _____

10. _____

11. _____

12. _____

3.10 Ciudades, pueblos y paisajes
Cities, Villages, and Landscapes

Take a good look at the landscape below. Fill in the blanks with the words provided.

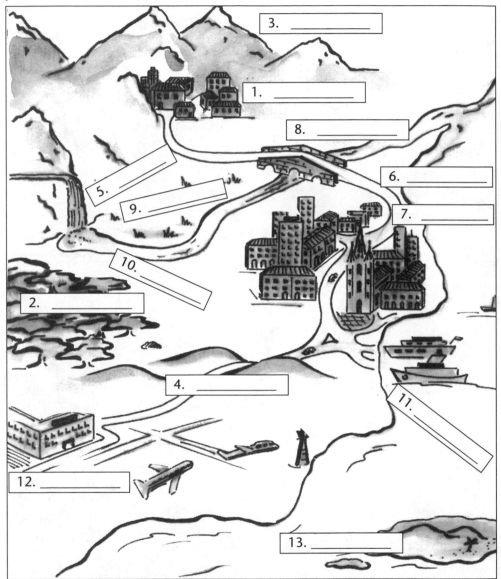

3. _____

1. _____

8. _____

5. _____

9. _____

6. _____

7. _____

10. _____

2. _____

4. _____

11. _____

12. _____

13. _____

el pueblo	la ciudad	el río	la montaña	el puente	la isla	el puerto
el bosque	la colina	la pradera	la cascada	la carretera		el aeropuerto

En la ciudad
In Town

Mark everything that you see in the picture.

¿Qué hay en la ciudad? En la ciudad hay . . .

1. ☐ un museo
2. ☐ un hospital
3. ☐ dos teatros
4. ☐ un parque
5. ☐ una plaza
6. ☐ gente
7. ☐ un supermercado
8. ☐ una escuela
9. ☐ una parada del autobús
10. ☐ casas
11. ☐ tres hoteles
12. ☐ un restaurante
13. ☐ una farmacia
14. ☐ dos bares
15. ☐ una catedral
16. ☐ una oficina de Correos
17. ☐ calles
18. ☐ una estación de metro
19. ☐ niños
20. ☐ coches
21. ☐ un semáforo

3.12 Medios de transporte
Means of Transportation

Drill 1

Match the means of transportation with the drawings.

la bicicleta	el taxi	el tren
el autobús	el camión	el avión
el coche	la moto	el barco

1. _____ 2. _____ 3. _____

4. _____ 5. _____ 6. _____

7. _____ 8. _____ 9. _____

Drill 2

Complete the following sentences with the correct terms.

avión   autobús   pie   barco   tren

1. En la estación se toma el _____ .   2. Cuando caminamos vamos a ____ .

3. En el puerto tomamos el _____ .   4. En la parada se toma el _____ .

5. Vamos al aeropuerto para viajar en _____ .

3.13 Medios de comunicación modernos
Modern Means of Communication

Match the sentences below with the drawings.

1. Mario saca dinero del cajero automático.
2. Hoy he recibido un fax de Uruguay.
3. Miguel está hablando por teléfono con su mujer.
4. Concha tiene un contestador automático.
5. José está trabajando en su ordenador.
6. Anita saca todas sus cuentas con una calculadora.

a. _____   b. _____   c. _____

d. _____   e. _____   f. _____

3.14 Tiendas
Stores

a) Where can you buy these products? Write the product names next to the appropriate shops.

leche	vestidos	botas	carne	revistas	sellos	pasteles
pan	manzanas	pescado	libros	zapatillas	jerseys	queso
arroz	vino	bolígrafos	mariscos	zapatos	faldas	peras
uvas	pantalones	sandalias	chuletas	gambas	periódicos	galletas

1. Supermercado _____*leche*_____

2. Zapatería _____

3. Panadería y pastelería _____

4. Boutique _____

5. Librería _____

6. Pescadería _____

7. Carnicería _____

8. Frutería _____

9. Estanco _____

b) At the shopping center—En el centro comercial: In which department would you buy these items? Match them with the correct categories.

A. Artículos electrodomésticos _____

B. Confección caballeros _____

C. Juguetería _____

D. Papelería _____

1. traje

2. televisor

5. papel para cartas

6. camisa

3. radio-casete

4. juguetes

3.15 Restaurante y bar
Restaurant and Bar

Using the dishes and beverages provided, put together your own menu.

gazpacho
filete con patatas fritas
zumo de naranja
flan
merluza a la romana
paella
tortilla española

ensalada mixta
macedonia de fruta
vino blanco
pollo al ajillo
sopa de verduras
helado
fruta

café
gambas a la plancha
chuletas con ensalada
pudín
cerveza
ensalada de lechuga
agua mineral

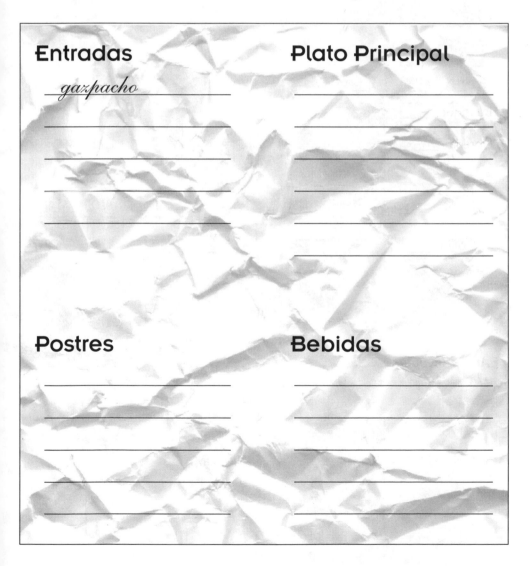

Entradas

gazpacho

_____

_____

_____

_____

Plato Principal

_____

_____

_____

_____

_____

Postres

_____

_____

_____

_____

Bebidas

_____

_____

_____

_____

Alimentos
Foods

Drill 1: Vegetables and Fruits

Match the foods with the pictures.

fresas	lechuga	coliflor	tomates	melón	naranja	sandía	uvas
manzana	limón	aceitunas	zanahoria	piña	patatas	pera	plátanos

1. _____

2. _____

3. _____

4. _____

5. _____

6. _____

7. _____

8. _____

9. _____

10. _____

11. _____

12. _____

13. _____

14. _____

15. _____

16. _____

Drill 2: Meat and Fish

Write the names of these foods under the appropriate pictures.

jamón   carne   salchichón   salchicha   pescado   pollo

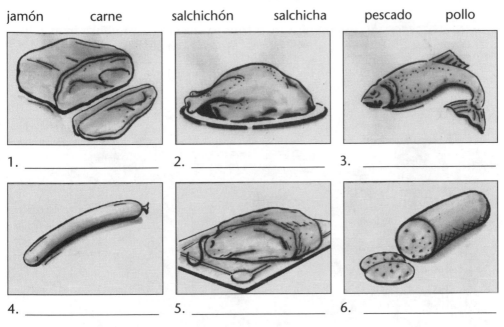

1. _____   2. _____   3. _____

4. _____   5. _____   6. _____

Drill 3: Staple Foods

Match the products with the drawings.

huevos   leche   pan   mantequilla   queso   harina

1. _____   2. _____   3. _____

4. _____   5. _____   6. _____

3.17 Las vacaciones
Vacation

The travel agency *"El cosmopolita"* lists trips to various destinations in its schedule. Where are the following people going? Match each person with a destination.

Costa del Sol	Pirineos	Suiza	La Mancha
Islas Canarias	París	Brasil	Andalucía

1. A María le gusta esquiar. _____

2. A Irene y Alberto les gusta el carnaval. _____

3. A Carmen le encanta bailar flamenco. _____

4. A Ana le gusta la playa y tomar el sol. _____

5. A Geles le gustan las islas. _____

6. Al señor Mendoza le gustan los museos. _____

7. A Pablo le gusta la montaña pero no le gusta salir fuera de España. _____

8. A la señora López le encantan los molinos de viento y el campo. _____

3.18 El dinero
Money

What do you say in the following situations? From the sentences provided, choose the one that best fits each of the situations described.

What do you say when you . . .

1. – ask where the bank is.

   ¿Dónde está el banco?

2. – would like to withdraw 20,000 pesetas from your account.

3. – ask what the exchange rate for the peseta is.

4. – want to know how much you have to pay for the ticket.

5. – ask where you can cash the check.

6. – accept eurocheques.

7. – write a check.

8. – want to know whether you can change 10,000 pesetas to dollars.

9. – want to know whether someone can change 1000 pesetas for you.

h. Se aceptan eurocheques.

b. ¿Dónde está el banco?

d. Quiero retirar veinte mil pesetas de mi cuenta.

i. ¿Cuánto cuesta el billete?

c. ¿Me puede cambiar mil pesetas en monedas?

e. Extiendo un cheque.

f. ¿Me puede cambiar diez mil pesetas en dólares?

a. ¿En qué banco puedo cobrar el cheque?

g. ¿A cómo está el cambio de la peseta?

3.19 El tiempo
Weather

"*Hacer*" is an important verb when you want to talk about the weather.

First, look at the pictures. Then read the sentences and write them under the appropriate pictures.

1. Hace buen tiempo.
   Hace sol.
   Tengo calor.

2. ¿Qué tiempo hace?
   Hace mal tiempo.
   Está lloviendo.

3. Hace frío.
   Está nevando.
   Tengo mucho frío.

4. Hace viento.
   Hay niebla.
   El tiempo está muy malo.

A _____

B _____

C _____

D _____

44

3.20 La hora
Time

How do you ask the time? ¿Qué hora es?
How do you give information about the time? Es la una./Son las tres.
How do you inquire about a particular time? ¿A qué hora vamos al cine?
How do you indicate a particular time? A la una./A las ocho.

Son las tres **en punto.** Son las tres **y cuarto.** Son las tres **y media.** Son las cuatro **menos** cuarto.

Write the time beneath each clock face.

1. _____

_____

2. _____

_____

3. _____

_____

4. _____

_____

5. _____

6. _____

7. _____

8. _____

9. _____

_____

10. _____

_____

11. _____

_____

12. _____

_____

Chapter 4

Formación de palabras
Word Formation

1. Words can be used to form new words.

Many words belong to a family, for example:

la cocina → cocinar → el cocinero → la cocinera.

2. Learn new words along with their families.

When you enter a new word into your vocabulary notebook, it's a good idea to look for its "relatives" in your dictionary and memorize them as well.

3. Form word families.

You'll learn a great many new terms by studying words as part of a family. In that way you can learn how new words can be formed.

4.1 Formación de adverbios
Adverb Formation

Adverbs can be derived from adjectives by adding *-mente* to the feminine form of the adjective.
For example:

afortunado	→	afortuna**mente**
fácil	→	fácil**mente**

Note: The adjective retains its written accent.

Change the following adjectives into adverbs.

1. actual   *actualmente* _____

2. adecuado _____

3. alegre _____

4. amable _____

5. amistoso _____

6. cómodo _____

7. corriente _____

8. desesperado _____

9. exacto _____

10. general _____

11. lento _____

12. peligroso _____

13. propio _____

14. suficiente _____

15. tradicional _____

16. difícil _____

4.2 Prefijos
Prefixes

New words can be formed with prefixes. Prefixes are syllables placed before a word or another prefix to create a new word. These prefixes occur frequently: *des-, in-, anti-*.

Which prefixes are likely to precede the words listed below? Fill in the blanks with des-, in, or anti-.

1. ___*des*___contento

2. _____ capaz

3. _____ autoritario

4. _____ conocido

5. _____ empleo

6. _____ dependiente

7. _____ comunista

8. _____ tolerante

9. _____ ventaja

10. _____ igual

11. _____ soportable

12. _____ cubrir

13. _____ terrorista

14. _____ esperado

4.3 Sustantivo y adjetivo
Noun and Adjective

Fill in the missing words by forming the correct adjectives.

1. la dificultad   *difícil* _____

2. la enfermedad _____

3. la importancia _____

4. la alegría _____

5. la posibilidad _____

4.4 Verbo y sustantivo
Verb and Noun

Fill in the missing words by forming the correct noun or verb.

Verbo	Sustantivo
1. _____	salida
2. visitar	_____
3. _____	información
4. reservar	_____
5. _____	desayuno
6. bañarse	_____
7. _____	llegada
8. ducharse	_____
9. _____	aparcamiento
10. preguntar	_____
11. parar	_____
12. nevar	_____
13. _____	perdón

4.5 Formación de sustantivos
Noun Formation

Drill 1

In Spanish, a great many compound nouns are formed with the preposition *"de."* For example, *una taza de café.*

Form compound nouns with the preposition "de."

1. una taza para tomar café _____una taza de café_____
2. una agencia que organiza viajes _____
3. una camisa hecha de algodón _____
4. un billete para viajar en avión _____
5. un vestido para la noche _____
6. un carnet que sirve para conducir _____
7. un instrumento que sirve para hacer música _____
8. un compañero que está en nuestra clase _____

Drill 2

Some compound nouns are formed with a noun and an adjective. One example: *una habitación doble.*

Form compound nouns by matching the adjectives with the appropriate nouns.

fotográfica	eléctrica	~~individual~~	industrial	completa

1. la habitación _____individual_____
2. la cocina _____
3. la cámara _____
4. la pensión _____
5. la ciudad _____

50

Chapter 5

Pronunciación y ortografía
Pronunciation and Spelling

1. Learn words and their pronunciation simultaneously.

Whenever you learn a new word, memorize its pronunciation and spelling at the same time.

2. Memorize the rules of pronunciation and spelling.

In good dictionaries, you will find the rules of Spanish pronunciation and spelling. Commit to memory the pronunciation of the letters that cause you the most trouble.

Pronunciación
Pronunciation

Keep in mind that
- c before e and i is pronounced [θ] in Spain, as is z, but [s] in Latin America, and
- g before e and i is pronounced like the "h" in house [x], as is j.

Enter the following words under the correct headings.

ciudad	cine	salchicha	gente	creer
mucho	viajar	domingo	hijo	leche
zapato	charlar	ganar	mujer	cuidado
quedar	ducha	jardín	poco	dulce
clase	gustar	agua	azul	gato

1. [θ] or [s]

2. [k]

3. [tʃ]

_____   _____   _____

_____   _____   _____

_____   _____   _____

_____   _____   _____

_____   _____   _____

4. [x]

5. [g]

_____   _____

_____   _____

_____   _____

_____   _____

_____   _____

5.2 Acentuación y entonación
Stress

Words of more than one syllable that end in a vowel, n, or s are stressed on the next to last syllable. Those that end in a consonant (other than n or s) are stressed on the last syllable. Exceptions to these two rules, including all words stressed on the third syllable from the last, are written with an accent mark.

Enter the following words in the blanks.

gafas	bocadillo	árbol	igual	comer
inteligente	comes	teléfono	cómodo	coger
libertad	época	tráfico	bolígrafo	nación

third syllable from the last	next to last syllable	last syllable
_____	*gafas* _____	_____
_____	_____	_____
_____	_____	_____
_____	_____	_____
_____	_____	_____

5.3 Acento
Written Accent

Which words are missing a written accent? Fill in the accent marks.

Juana y José viven en una pequeña granja en Panama. Son campesinos. Todos los dias tienen que levantarse muy temprano para realizar las labores de la pequeña granja y llevar a los niños a la escuela. Tienen dos niños, Jaime que tiene 8 años y está en el segundo grado y Teresa que tiene 11 años y está en el cuarto grado. José va todos los sabados al mercado para vender la mercancia. Cultivan tomates, platanos y otras legumbres. Despues de vender la mercancia, regresa a casa generalmente muy tarde. A veces, no puede vender todo y el resto lo guarda para el consumo en casa o para venderlo la proxima semana.

Chapter 6

Combinaciones de palabras
Word Combinations

1. Many words belong together.

It's helpful to learn words in "partnerships." In Spanish, for example, people say:

> *hacer las maletas*

while in English, we say

> *to pack the bags.*

2. Memorize vocabulary in word combinations.

Certain words change their meaning when they appear in combination with other words. Verbs in particular often change their meaning when they are used with other prepositions or reflexive pronouns, as in these examples:

dejar	*to leave; to let,*
dejar de	*to shop,*
dejarse	*to be slovenly.*

Verbos con diferentes significados
Verbs with Different Meanings

Use these verbs with the appropriate prepositions and adjuncts, if necessary, to complete the sentences below. Don't forget to conjugate the verbs.

contar to count	**pensar en** to think of
contar con to rely on	**pensar** + *inf* to intend
dejar to lend	**poner** to put, place, lay
dejar de + *inf* to stop	**ponerse** to become, get
hablar con to talk with	**quedar bien** to suit
hablar de to talk about	**quedarse** to stay

1. A mi hermano le gusta mucho ___*hablar de*___ política.

2. Este vestido te _____ muy bien.

3. ¿Quién_____ los libros en la mesa?

4. Si _____ llover, voy a ir de paseo.

5. ¿Me _____ (tú) dos mil pesetas?

6. En el banco los empleados _____ los billetes todos los días.

7. Quiero _____ mi madre.

8. ¿Puedo _____ la ayuda de Ana para organizar la fiesta?

9. Mis amigos _____ ir de vacaciones en julio.

10. _____ en casa.

11. Josefina siempre _____ ti.

12. Al oír la noticia, Sonia _____ muy triste.

6.2 Verbos útiles
Useful Verbs

Fill in the blanks with the appropriate verbs.

decir   hacer   llevar   hablar   ver   buscar

estar

escuchar   ir   cerrar   pasar   tener

poner   tomar   jugar   valer   romperse   dar

1. _cerrar_ la puerta

2. _____ un brazo

3. _____ deporte

4. _____ un paseo

5. _____ de acuerdo

6. _____ al fútbol

7. _____ la radio

8. _____ la televisión

9. _____ suerte

10. _____ la verdad

11. _____ la mesa

12. _____ en tren

13. _____ trabajo

14. _____ una decisión

15. _____ la pena

16. _____ español

17. _____ un examen

18. _____ gafas

Assign the verbs to the correct groups.

estar   tomar   tener   hacer   ir   ser

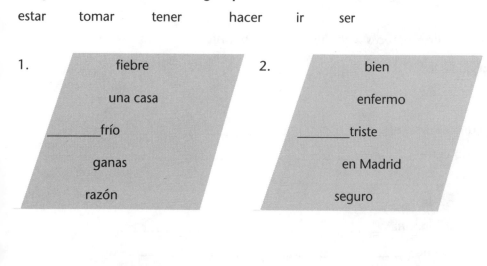

1.
fiebre

una casa

_____frío

ganas

razón

2.
bien

enfermo

_____triste

en Madrid

seguro

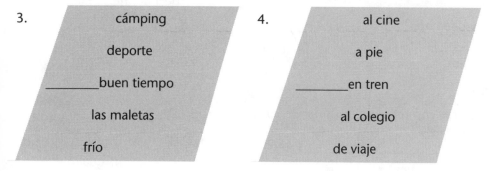

3.
cámping

deporte

_____buen tiempo

las maletas

frío

4.
al cine

a pie

_____en tren

al colegio

de viaje

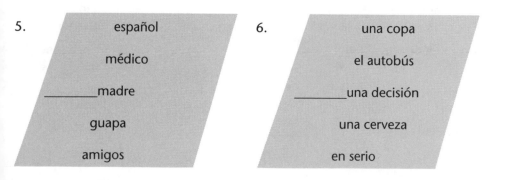

5.
español

médico

_____madre

guapa

amigos

6.
una copa

el autobús

_____una decisión

una cerveza

en serio

6.4 Verbos + sustantivos, adjetivos y adverbios

Verbs + Nouns, Adjectives, and Adverbs

Drill 1

Complete the sentences with the following nouns.

posibilidades	duda	favor	importancia
ganas	acuerdo	pena	verdad

1. Lo que tú dices es_____ .

2. Eso no tiene _____ .

3. Me da_____ .

4. No estoy de _____ .

5. No cabe ninguna _____ .

6. Me hace un _____ .

7. No tengo _____ de ir al cine.

8. Hay diferentes _____ .

Drill 2

Choose the correct word to complete each sentence.

1. ¡Me da _____!

   a. igual
   b. igualmente

2. ¡Me gusta _____!

   a. muy
   b. mucho

3. Carmen es muy _____ .

   a. guapa
   b. enferma

4. Pepe conduce muy _____ .

   a. bien
   b. bueno

5. ¿Puedes hablar más _____ , por favor?

   a. despacio
   b. lento

6. Pedro es muy gordo. Come _____ .

   a. mucho
   b. poco

Qué + sustantivo, adjetivo y adverbio

Qué + *Noun, Adjective, and Adverb*

Qué + noun, adjective, and adverb is used to express feelings and states of mind.

Choose the word that correctly completes the sentence.

1. ¡Qué _____ de verte!

   a. alegre

   b. alegría

2. ¡Qué _____ está la paella!

   a. pobre

   b. rica

3. ¡Qué _____ está María!

   a. feliz

   b. felicidad

4. Mira esa ciudad. ¡Qué _____ !

   a. bonita

   b. buena

5. Mira ese chico. ¡Qué _____ !

   a. guapa

   b. guapo

6. Ha perdido a su madre. ¡Qué_____ !

   a. malo

   b. triste

7. No tengo tiempo. ¡Qué _____ !

   a. mal

   b. lástima

8. ¡Qué _____ tiempo hace!

   a. bien

   b. buen

9. ¡Qué _____ estoy hoy!

   a. contento

   b. estupendo

10. ¡Qué _____ idea!

   a. buena

   b. bueno

Chapter 7

Situaciones
Situations

1. Expand your vocabulary relative to specific situations.

Memorize words that you need in order to react appropriately in certain situations.

2. Complete sentences make communication easier.

Learn sentences that are specific to a certain situation, so that you can carry on every-day conversations with ease. Sentences like *¿Qué tal?* or *¡Buenos días!* will quickly become fixed in your memory once you have used them.

3. Turns of speech are important in conversations.

Fixed expressions can be very important. Memorizing standardized sentences will make it easier for you to respond as the situation demands.

7.1 Saludo y despedida
Saying Hello and Good-bye

a) Put the following sentences in the correct column.

1. ¡Buenos días!   2. ¡Hasta mañana!   3. Hola, ¿qué tal?   4. ¡Adiós, hasta pronto!
5. ¡Buenas tardes!   6. ¡Buenas noches!   7. ¡Hasta el lunes!   8. ¡Hasta luego!

Hello	Good-bye
¡Buenos días!	_____
_____	_____
_____	_____
_____	_____
	_____

b) Complete the following dialogues with the words provided.

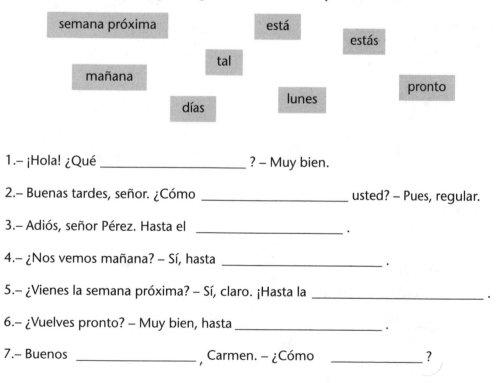

semana próxima   está   estás   tal   mañana   días   lunes   pronto

1.– ¡Hola! ¿Qué _____ ? – Muy bien.

2.– Buenas tardes, señor. ¿Cómo _____ usted? – Pues, regular.

3.– Adiós, señor Pérez. Hasta el _____ .

4.– ¿Nos vemos mañana? – Sí, hasta _____ .

5.– ¿Vienes la semana próxima? – Sí, claro. ¡Hasta la _____ .

6.– ¿Vuelves pronto? – Muy bien, hasta _____ .

7.– Buenos _____ , Carmen. – ¿Cómo _____ ?

Encontrarse

Arranging to Meet

Drill 1: Arranging to meet and expressing invitations

Complete the dialogues with the verbs provided. Make an "x" to indicate whether the invitation is accepted or declined.

~~Tomamos~~   gustaría   Vamos   venir   venís   Vienen

	Accepted	Declined
1. – ¿ _Tomamos_ un café? – Sí, con mucho gusto.	X	
2. – ¿ _____ al cine? – Lo siento, pero no puedo.		
3. – ¿Quieres _____ a mi casa para la cena? – Vale.		
4. – Hola, chicos, ¿ _____ conmigo a tomar algo? – Sí, perfecto.		
5. – ¿ _____ ustedes a la ópera con nosotros? – Nos gustaría, pero no podemos.		
6. Me_____ invitarte al restaurante. – Gracias, pero no tengo tiempo.		

Drill 2: Agreeing on a place and time

Choose the correct answer.

1. ¿Dónde quedamos?   a. ☐ A mi casa.   b. ☐ En mi casa.

2. ¿Cuándo quedamos?   a. ☐ Dentro de media hora.   b. ☐ En casa.

3. ¿Dónde nos vemos?   a. ☐ Delante del cine.   b. ☐ A las nueve y media.

4. ¿A qué hora nos vemos?   a. ☐ A las ocho.   b. ☐ Son las ocho.

5. ¿Cuándo vamos de paseo?   a. ☐ Al fin de semana.   b. ☐ El fin de semana.

Al teléfono
On the Telephone

Complete the dialogues with the words provided. Remember that in Spanish, too, the first word of each sentence is capitalized.

Word bank (telephone illustration): soy, hablo, quién, el, hasta, con, a, puedo, momento, parte, día, por, bien, está, necesito, desea, siento, órdenes, quién, tarde

1. ● Buenos días ¿ ____*está*____ Marta?

   ▲ ¿ _____ la llama?

   ● _____ María.

   ▲ Sí, un _____ , por favor.

2. ● ¿_____ con el consultorio del doctor Pérez?

   ▲ Sí, ¿qué _____ ?

   ● _____ una cita.

   ▲ Está bien. ¿Qué _____ puede usted?

   ● _____ lunes _____ la tarde.

   ▲ Muy _____ , el lunes_____ las 2.30.

   ● Gracias, _____ el lunes.

3. ● Buenos días, ¿hablo _____ la empresa Laresa?

   ▲ Sí, a sus _____ .

   ● ¿_____ hablar con el señor González, por favor?

   ▲ ¿De parte de _____ ?

   ● De _____ de la señora García.

   ▲ Lo _____ , en este momento se encuentra en una reunión.

   Llame más _____ .

En una fiesta
At a Party

Complete the dialogues with the sentences given below.

a. Me llamo Ernesto. b. ¡Hola, qué simpáticos! c. Sí, soy Elena Pérez.
d. Encantado. Y yo soy Miguel. e. Soy de Barcelona. f. Muy bien, ¿y tú?

En la estación y en el aeropuerto

At the Train Station and at the Airport

Drill 1: En la estación

Complete the sentences with the words supplied below.

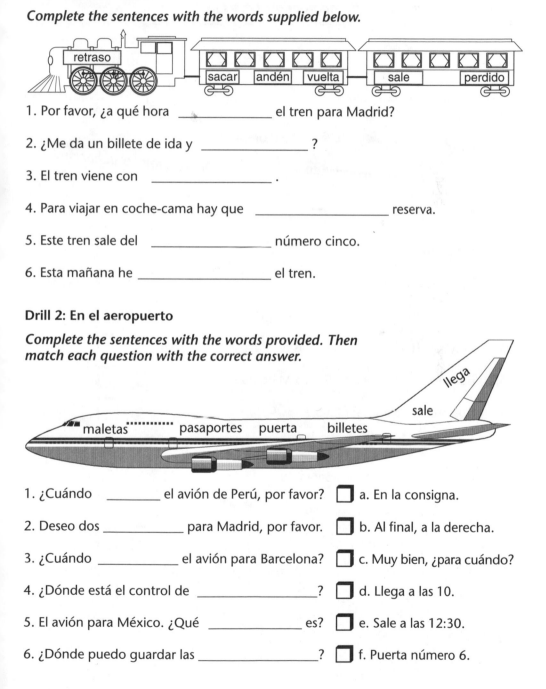

1. Por favor, ¿a qué hora _____ el tren para Madrid?

2. ¿Me da un billete de ida y _____ ?

3. El tren viene con _____ .

4. Para viajar en coche-cama hay que _____ reserva.

5. Este tren sale del _____ número cinco.

6. Esta mañana he _____ el tren.

Drill 2: En el aeropuerto

Complete the sentences with the words provided. Then match each question with the correct answer.

1. ¿Cuándo _____ el avión de Perú, por favor?   ☐ a. En la consigna.

2. Deseo dos _____ para Madrid, por favor.   ☐ b. Al final, a la derecha.

3. ¿Cuándo _____ el avión para Barcelona?   ☐ c. Muy bien, ¿para cuándo?

4. ¿Dónde está el control de _____ ?   ☐ d. Llega a las 10.

5. El avión para México. ¿Qué _____ es?   ☐ e. Sale a las 12:30.

6. ¿Dónde puedo guardar las _____ ?   ☐ f. Puerta número 6.

7.6 De compras
Going Shopping

In what shops will you hear the following sentences? Match the sentences with the shops or stores and write the appropriate letters in the boxes.

h. en la oficina de

e. *en la zapatería*

b. en la librería

i. *en la panadería*

d. en el estanco

f. *en la farmacia*

a. *en la juguetería*

g. **en la papelería**

c. **en el supermercado**

j. *en los grandes almacenes*

1. ¿Tiene usted pantalones? [j]

2. Una caja de aspirinas, por favor. [ ]

3. Deseo una muñeca para una niña de 10 años. [ ]

4. La revista „Hola" y unas cajetillas de cigarrillos, por favor. [ ]

5. ¿Tienen el último libro de García Márquez? [ ]

6. ¿Qué número calza, por favor? [ ]

7. ¿Dónde están los carritos para la compra? [ ]

8. ¿Cuánto cuesta una carta para Estados Unidos? [ ]

9. Déme diez panecillos, por favor. [ ]

10. ¿Tiene papel de carta? [ ]

7.7 En el mercado
At the Market

a) Complete the dialogue with the words provided.

medio	son	desea	Cómo	Póngame
todo	Algo	maduros	Tenga	cuánto

Vendedor: 1. Buenos días. ¿Qué _____?

Cliente: 2. _____ un kilo de tomates, por favor.

Vendedor: 3. ¿_____ los quiere?

Cliente: 4. Bien _____ , son para una salsa.

Vendedor: 5. ¿_____ más?

Cliente: 6. Sí, _____ kilo de patatas.

Vendedor: 7. ¿Es _____?

Cliente: 8. Sí, ¿_____ es?

Vendedor: 9. _____ 550 pts.

Cliente: 10. _____ . Adiós, señor.

b) Mrs. Menéndez is shopping at the market. Play the role of Mrs. Menéndez and ask for the things on the shopping list.

Déme

1 kg fresas

1/2 kg zanahorias

2 kg naranjas

1 piña

_____

_____

_____

_____

7.8 Pedir la comida
Ordering a Meal

Drill 1

Put these sentences into the correct order.

Mario y Gabriela van a un restaurante.

☐	*Camarero:*	a.	¿Qué desean tomar los señores?
☐	*Mario:*	b.	¿Tomamos una botella de vino rosado juntos?
☐	*Mario:*	c.	Para mí un helado de chocolate y la cuenta, por favor.
☐	*Camarero:*	d.	¿Y para beber?
☐	*Gabriela:*	e.	Para mí un flan. ¿Y tú, Mario?
☑	*Camarero:*	f.	Buenas noches. ¿Les gusta esta mesa?
☐	*Gabriela:*	g.	No, prefiero vino blanco.
☐	*Mario:*	h.	Para mí, de primero una sopa del día y de segundo filete con patatas fritas.
☐	*Mario:*	i.	Entonces, una botella de medio litro rosado y una de medio litro blanco.
☐	*Mario:*	j.	Sí, está muy bien. La carta, por favor.
☐	*Gabriela:*	k.	Y yo, de primero gazpacho y de segundo gambas a la plancha.
☐	*Camarero:*	l.	¿Desean postre?

Drill 2

What does the guest ask the waiter for? Complete the sentences with the words supplied below.

cuchara   azúcar   tinto   cerveza

1. Una   *cuchara*   , por favor.

2. Un poco de   _____ , por favor.

3. Otra   _____ , por favor.

4. Otro   _____ , por favor.

7.9 Preguntar el camino

Asking for Directions

Drill 1

Match the directions with the pictures, and write the letter denoting each building in the correct box.

a. ● ¿Dónde está el museo?

  ▲ Tiene que seguir todo recto hasta el semáforo. Detrás del semáforo a la derecha está el museo.

b. ● ¿Dónde está el hotel?

  ▲ Tiene que cruzar la plaza y, después de la plaza, la primera a la izquierda y al final a la izquierda.

c. ● ¿Dónde está el banco?

  ▲ Tiene que seguir recto, la segunda calle tuerza a la derecha y en la esquina a la izquierda allí está el banco.

1 __

2 __

3 __

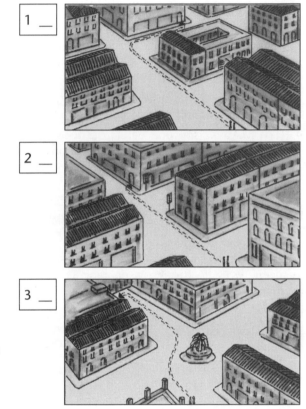

Drill 2

Complete the sentences with the words given below.

está	perdone	hay	librería	puedo	enfrente

1. _____ , ¿dónde _____ el hotel Cervantes?

2. ¿ _____ una farmacia por aquí?

3. Oiga, ¿dónde _____ tomar el autobús número 5?

4. ¿Sabe usted si hay una _____ cerca?

5. Por favor, ¿hay un estanco _____ del hotel?

7.10 Ir de vacaciones
Going on Vacation

Read what these people would like to do on vacation. Which travel agency offers suitable trips for which people?

1. La familia Ramos tiene tres niños. Desean pasar sus vacaciones cerca del mar. Quieren alquilar una casa vacacional.

2. Carlos y Alberto son estudiantes y les gustaría hacer un viaje barato. No les gustaría alojarse en hoteles o pensiones. Les gusta el contacto con la naturaleza y con personas de su misma edad.

3. A Andrés y a Marta les gustan mucho los deportes y los viajes de aventuras. También les gusta tener contacto con la naturaleza.

4. Los Martínez son una pareja de unos 50 años. A ellos les gustan los viajes en grupo y hacer visitas a museos y a monumentos importantes.

A _____

Agencia de viajes Trotamundos

¿Le gusta hacer alpinismo? ¿Hacer excursiones en las montañas? Ofrecemos vacaciones en los Pirineos españoles. Dos semanas en contacto con la naturaleza practicando alpinismo de montaña.

Llame hoy mismo: Tel. 34565

B _____

Viajes La Seguridad

Ofrecemos viajes para familias en casas vacacionales para 5 o más personas. La playa está sólo a 600 metros. Las casas están cerca de campos de juegos para niños.

Reserve con tiempo por teléfono.

Tlf 617687   Fax 4617689

C _____

Agencia Francia

París en una semana.
Conozca una de las ciudades más interesantes de Europa. Tenemos viajes organizados en grupo. Hacemos visitas guiadas a los monumentos más interesantes de París.

Tlf 987345

D _____

Agencia La Comodidad

Nuestros viajes son especialmente organizados para estudiantes, ofrecemos alojamientos, albergues de juventud o reservas para tiendas de campaña. Podemos organizar viajes en grupos pequeños o individuales a partir de dos personas. ¡Llámanos!

Nuestro número telefónico: 243675

7.11 En el hotel
At the Hotel

Form sentences with the words provided.

1. habitación – con – doble – deseo – una – ducha.

   _____

2. quiero – una – para – reservar – tres – días – habitación.

   _____

3. de – llaves – las – favor – la – por – habitación.

   _____

4. ¿el – dónde – por – está – favor – ascensor?

   _____

5. ¿desean – días – cuántos – pasar – aquí?

   _____

6. ¿da – tienen – habitación – una – que – al – patio?

   _____

7. la – déme – por – cuenta – favor.

   _____

8. para – una – con – dos – habitación – ducha – personas.

   _____

9. ¿el – dónde – comedor – favor – está – por?

   _____

10. ¿llamar – por – puedo – favor – por – teléfono?

   _____

11. quedamos – el 18 – desde – nos – el 30 – hasta.

   _____

12. ¿el – hay – en – piscina – hotel?

   _____

7.12 Un turista en Hispanoamérica
A Tourist in Latin America

There are differences between the Spanish spoken in Spain and that spoken in Latin America, particularly in regard to vocabulary. For some things, different words are used, and some words have an entirely different meaning in Latin America. Within the Latin American countries, too, there are differences in language.

On the left, we have written the sentences you would hear in Latin America. What would be the Castilian Spanish version of the words in boldface? We have provided the words commonly used in Spain in the right-hand column. Make the correct matches.

1. Este **tinto** está muy caliente.
2. ¿Me da un kilo de **papas**?
3. ¿A qué hora viene **la guagua**?
4. Déme **una estampilla** de dos pesos.
5. Aquí tiene los **boletos** de avión.
6. Esta **pollera** me queda muy larga.
7. Camarero, un **jugo** de naranja, por favor.
8. Mi hermano tiene **mucha plata**.
9. Pónte el **suéter**, que está haciendo frío.
10. ¿Quieres un **bocadillo de guayaba**?
11. Deseo un **sándwich** de jamón.
12. ¿Dónde puedo **tomar** el autobús?
13. Déme un kilo de **damascos**.
14. ¿De qué año es tu **carro**?

a. bocadillo
b. café negro
c. falda
d. patatas
e. mucho dinero
f. billetes
g. un sello
h. albaricoques
i. zumo
j. dulce de guayaba
k. el autobús
l. coche
m. jersey
n. coger

1. _b_	2. ___	3. ___	4. ___	5. ___	6. ___	7. ___
8. ___	9. ___	10. ___	11. ___	12. ___	13. ___	14. ___

7.13 Casos de urgencia
Emergencies

First, read the information in English. Then help Mr. Smith fill out the form.

Mr. Smith's car was stolen in front of a shopping center in Barcelona.
Harold Smith had a gray Ford, model year 2001, with a plate reading M – XS 5485.
The theft occurred at 3 P.M.
The American is presently a guest at the hotel "La Palma," Calle Solana No. 57.

Nombre _____

Apellido _____

Dirección _____

Nacionalidad _____

Objeto robado _____

Color _____

Marca _____

Año _____

Lugar del robo _____

_____

Hora del robo _____

7.14 Alquilar una vivienda
Renting an Apartment

After reading the following passage, help the Rodríguez family find an apartment. Mark the most suitable apartment with an "x."

La familia Rodríguez tiene dos niños. Van a vivir en Valencia y buscan vivienda. Ellos sólo pueden pagar 150.000 pesetas al mes y quieren un piso cerca de la escuela en el centro. Tienen coche.

1.

Se alquila piso en las afueras de Valencia. Un dormitorio, salón-comedor, cocina equipada, garaje, ducha y un pequeño jardín.

Alquiler 200.000 pts. al mes.

2.

Alquilo piso, 4 dormitorios, salón-comedor, cocina equipada, dos baños.
Cerca del centro. Dos garajes.
Alquiler 380.000 pts.

3.

Se alquila casa pequeña a diez kilómetros de Valencia, 3 dormitorios, salón-comedor grande, baño, cocina completa y jardín.
Alquiler 150.000 pts.

4.

Se alquila piso totalmente renovado, 3 dormitorios, salón–comedor, cocina, baño pequeño, garaje. Alquiler 145.000 pts.

En el consultorio

At the Doctor's Office

Drill 1

Complete the dialogue with the words provided.

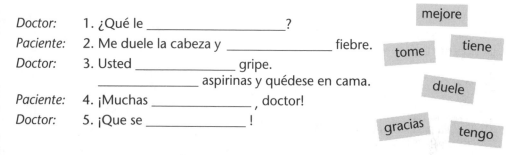

Doctor:	1. ¿Qué le _____?
Paciente:	2. Me duele la cabeza y _____ fiebre.
Doctor:	3. Usted _____ gripe.
	_____ aspirinas y quédese en cama.
Paciente:	4. ¡Muchas _____ , doctor!
Doctor:	5. ¡Que se _____ !

mejore

tome   tiene

duele

gracias   tengo

Drill 2

¿Qué le pasa?
Match the sentences with the pictures.

1. Le duele el brazo. 2. Le duele la garganta. 3. Le duele la pierna. 4. Tiene gripe.

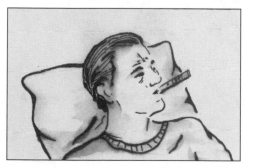

a. _____

b. _____

c. _____

d. _____

Buscar un empleo
Looking for a Job

Read the want ads, and then mark the statements that apply in each case.

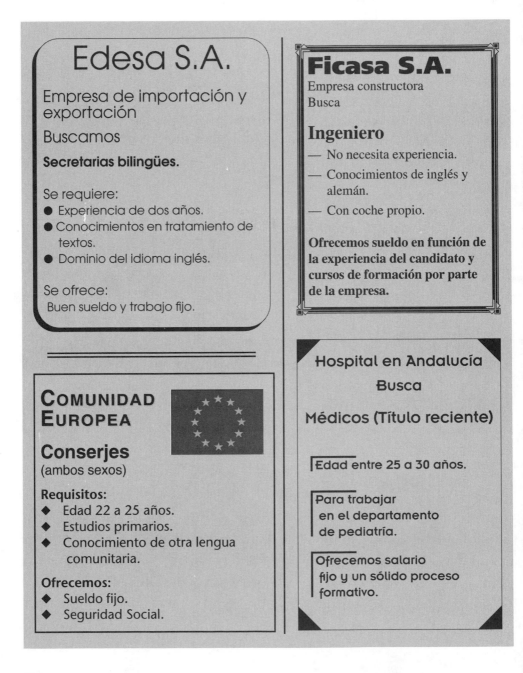

Edesa S.A.

Empresa de importación y exportación

Buscamos

Secretarias bilingües.

Se requiere:
● Experiencia de dos años.
● Conocimientos en tratamiento de textos.
● Dominio del idioma inglés.

Se ofrece:
 Buen sueldo y trabajo fijo.

Ficasa S.A.

Empresa constructora
Busca

Ingeniero

— No necesita experiencia.
— Conocimientos de inglés y alemán.
— Con coche propio.

Ofrecemos sueldo en función de la experiencia del candidato y cursos de formación por parte de la empresa.

COMUNIDAD EUROPEA

Conserjes
(ambos sexos)

Requisitos:
◆ Edad 22 a 25 años.
◆ Estudios primarios.
◆ Conocimiento de otra lengua comunitaria.

Ofrecemos:
◆ Sueldo fijo.
◆ Seguridad Social.

Hospital en Andalucía
Busca

Médicos (Título reciente)

Edad entre 25 a 30 años.

Para trabajar en el departamento de pediatría.

Ofrecemos salario fijo y un sólido proceso formativo.

1. Edesa S.A. es una
   - ☐ a. empresa constructora.
   - ☐ b. empresa de importación y exportación.

2. Edesa S.A. busca
   - ☐ a. un ingeniero.
   - ☐ b. secretarias.
   - ☐ c. secretarias con dominio del idioma inglés.

3. Edesa S.A. requiere
   - ☐ a. conocimientos de otra lengua comunitaria.
   - ☐ b. conocimientos en tratamiento de textos.

4. Edesa S.A. ofrece
   - ☐ a. sueldo en función de la experiencia.
   - ☐ b. buen sueldo.
   - ☐ c. salario fijo y altas comisiones.

5. Ficasa S.A. busca
   - ☐ a. un hombre con experiencia.
   - ☐ b. una mujer sin experiencia.
   - ☐ c. un hombre sin experiencia.

6. El ingeniero necesita
   - ☐ a. tener experiencia de dos años.
   - ☐ b. tener 25 años.
   - ☐ c. tener conocimientos de inglés y alemán.
   - ☐ d. tener coche propio.

7. El hospital busca
   - ☐ a. médicos con mucha experiencia.
   - ☐ b. médicos que tengan entre 25 a 30 años.
   - ☐ c. médicos con conocimientos de inglés.

8. La Comunidad Europea ofrece
   - ☐ a. buen sueldo.
   - ☐ b. sueldo fijo.
   - ☐ c. sueldo en función de la experiencia del candidato.
   - ☐ d. formación por parte de la Comunidad Europea.
   - ☐ e. Seguridad Social.

Chapter 8

Gramática
Grammar

1. Grammatical rules are important tools for learning a language.

To be able to put words together into a sentence, you need grammatical rules. Always memorize grammatical constructions together with sample sentences, so that you can fix the rules of grammar more firmly in your memory.

2. Practice new grammar as you learn it.

To have an active command of the language and use grammatical constructions correctly, you need to practice.

3. Verb conjugations are important in Spanish.

Since personal pronouns usually are omitted in Spanish, it is important to be able to conjugate verbs, so that you can understand others and make yourself understood as well.

For example: *Trabajamos en Madrid.*   We work in Madrid.
You can identify the subject of the verb only by the ending *–amos*

4. Grammar in your daily life.

Using a large sheet of paper, write out grammatical rules in the form of illustrative sentences or verb conjugations. Hang the sheet in parts of your apartment or house that you spend time in every day, such as the bathroom or the kitchen. Read through the constructions on a daily basis. After a certain time, you will have committed the rules and verb forms to memory with ease.

El sustantivo y sus acompañantes

The Noun and Its Companions

Remember that nouns that end in *-o, -aje, -ema, -oma, -ama, -l, -r,* and *-ón* are masculine. For example: *el paisaje, el problema, el idioma, el telegrama, el árbol, el lugar, el millón.*

Nouns with these endings are feminine: *-a, -d, -ión,* and *-z.*

For example: *la casa, la ciudad, la unión, la comunicación, la vez.*

There are also nouns that end in *-ista.* Most of them are both masculine and feminine: *el/la turista.*

There are exceptions as well, for example: *la foto, la radio, el día, el colega, el arroz.*

Fill in the definite and indefinite articles in the singular, and then put the noun together with the definite article in the plural.

	Article/Singular		Article/Plural
indefinite	definite		definite + noun
1. *un*	*el*	periódico	*los periódicos*
2. _____	_____	programa	_____
3. _____	_____	ciudad	_____
4. _____	_____	región	_____
5. _____	_____	solución	_____
6. _____	_____	libro	_____
7. _____	_____	casa	_____
8. _____	_____	bolso	_____
9. _____	_____	avión	_____
10. _____	_____	vez	_____
11. _____	_____	nacionalidad	_____
12. _____	_____	compañera	_____
13. _____	_____	accidente	_____
14. _____	_____	traje	_____

8.2 Sustantivo y adjetivo
Noun and Adjective

In Spanish, the number and gender of adjectives are determined by the noun they modify.

Adjectives usually follow the noun.

Certain adjectives always precede the noun: *mucho, poco, tanto, and otro.*

Malo, bueno, and *grande* can precede the noun. If they do so, *malo* and *bueno* lose the ending -o, and *grande* is shortened to *gran* and takes on the meaning "grand, magnificent":

(tener)	**mal**	gusto	un	**gran**	viaje
un	**buen**	amigo	una	**gran**	señora.

Drill 1

Mark the correct position for each adjective.

1. buen   ❏ tiempo ❏
2. interesantes   unos ❏ libros ❏
3. malo   un ❏ coche ❏
4. gran   un ❏ libro ❏
5. antipático   el ❏ jefe ❏
6. moderna   una ❏ escuela ❏
7. amable   el ❏ señor ❏
8. pocas   ❏ personas ❏
9. barato   un ❏ viaje ❏
10. mucho   ❏ dinero ❏
11. grande   una ❏ ciudad ❏
12. chilena   una ❏ escritora ❏

Drill 2

Complete the sentences with the adjectives provided.

buena	caros	industrial	bonitas	española	difícil

1. María y yo vivimos en una ciudad _____ .

2. Hemos comprado una nevera de _____ calidad.

3. Los vinos franceses son muy _____ .

4. Es un idioma muy _____ .

5. La cocina _____ me gusta mucho.

6. Las playas del Caribe son muy_____ .

8.3 Muy, mucho y poco

Muy, mucho, *and* poco.

Keep in mind that *muy,* in the sense of "very," always precedes the noun. *Mucho,* however, when used as an adverb must follow the verb. When used as an adjective of quantity, meaning "much, a great deal of," it is placed in front of the noun.

a) Complete the sentences with muy, mucho, mucha, muchos, *or* muchas.

1. María tiene _____ buenos amigos.

2. Desde que vive en Madrid, Juan tiene _____ amigos.

3. Hoy he comido _____ .

4. Juan y Carmen han hecho _____ viajes juntos.

5. Hoy hace _____ buen tiempo.

6. En Alemania se comen _____ manzanas.

7. En Italia el vino es _____ barato.

8. María bebe _____ leche.

b) Complete the sentences with poco, poca, pocos, *or* pocas.

1. En verano llueve _____ .

2. Voy _____ veces al cine.

3. Petra hace una dieta y come _____ .

4. Tengo _____ tiempo.

5. Esta habitación tiene _____ luz.

6. Hay _____ restaurantes por aquí.

c) Mark the correct position for the words below.

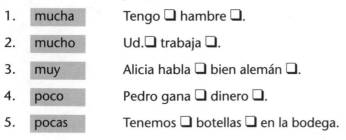

1. mucha   Tengo ❑ hambre ❑.

2. mucho   Ud.❑ trabaja ❑.

3. muy   Alicia habla ❑ bien alemán ❑.

4. poco   Pedro gana ❑ dinero ❑.

5. pocas   Tenemos ❑ botellas ❑ en la bodega.

8.4 Adjetivo o adverbio
Adjective or Adverb

 Remember that *alto, bajo, barato,* and *caro* do not have a separate adverb form.
For example: *Pepe habla* **alto/bajo.**
Esta falda es **cara/barata.**

Adjective or adverb?
Complete the sentences with the correct form of the adjective or with the adverb.

1. Es algo que no me interesa _____ .	personal
2. Ha hecho un examen muy _____ .	difícil
3. El conductor conduce _____ .	rápido
4. Lo que dices es _____ .	cierto
5. Eso es_____ imposible.	real
6. _____ vengo mañana a visitarte.	posible
7. Pedro llega siempre _____ .	puntual
8. Esa lección es muy _____ .	fácil
9. El tren es muy _____ .	rápido
10. El jefe es muy_____ .	simpático
11. Este niño aprende_____ .	fácil
12. La casa es muy _____ .	barato
13. José habla _____ .	lento
14. Compro siempre zumos _____ .	natural
15. ¿Puedes hablar más _____ , por favor?	alto
16. Este coche es muy _____ .	caro
17. Antonio es más _____ que su padre.	bajo
18. Carlos habla siempre muy _____ .	bajo

Los verbos regulares
Regular Verbs

a) Fill in the missing verb forms.

Infinitiv	yo	tú	el / ella usted	nosotros nosotras	vosotros vosotras	ellos / ellas ustedes
1. *trabajar*		*trabajas*				*trabajan*
2.	*bebo*			*bebemos*		
3.		*vives*			*vivís*	

b) Complete the sentences with the verbs provided. Don't forget to conjugate the verbs.

1. El profesor _____ las preguntas. **contestar**

2. Vosotros _____ muy bien italiano. **hablar**

3. ¿_____ una cerveza juntos? **beber**

4. ¿A quién _____ (tú) esa carta? **escribir**

5. Hoy (yo) _____ una llamada de mi padre. **recibir**

6. José _____ a su hijo en los deberes. **ayudar**

7. ¿Qué libro _____ (tú) ahora? **leer**

8. Nosotros _____ nuestra casa este año. **vender**

9. Ellos _____ en Barcelona ahora. **vivir**

10. ¿Qué _____ tu hermana en Valencia? **estudiar**

8.6 Los verbos irregulares
Irregular Verbs

Drill 1: Radical changing verbs with a vowel change in the stem from e to ie

pensar	
p**ie**nso	pensamos
p**ie**nsas	pensáis
p**ie**nsa	p**ie**nsan

This group also includes:
comenzar, despertar, empezar, entender, pensar, preferir, querer, sentir.

Complete the sentences with the verb forms provided.

empezáis   piensas   prefieres   quieren   entiende   siento   entendemos

1. ¿En qué _____ tú?

2. Usted _____ español, ¿verdad?

3. ¿María y Alfonso, _____ a trabajar ahora?

4. ¿_____ café o té?

5. Este año Jaime y Javier _____ ir de vacaciones a España.

6. Lo _____ mucho.

7. Nosotros _____ alemán.

Drill 2: Radical changing verbs with a vowel change in the stem from o to ue, u to ue

volver	
v**ue**lvo	volvemos
v**ue**lves	volvéis
v**ue**lve	v**ue**lven

This group also includes:
contar, costar, devolver, doler, dormir, morir, poder, recordar, volar.

jugar	
j**ue**go	jugamos
j**ue**gas	jugáis
j**ue**ga	j**ue**gan

Complete the sentences with the correct form of the verbs.

1. ¿Cuánto _____ esos bolígrafos?   costar

2. Mi tío _____ esta tarde del viaje.   volver

3. ¿Ana, _____ ayudarme, por favor?   poder

4. Los niños _____ .   dormir

5. Me _____ la muela.   doler

6. Los martes, nosotros _____ al tenis.   jugar

84

Drill 3

Tener, decir, oír, salir, and *hacer* end in *-go* in the first person singular.

Pablo is conducting a survey for a public opinion research institute, and at the moment he is interviewing Mr. Aguirre. Complete Mr. Aguirre's answers.

1. *Pablo:* ¿Tiene teléfono?

   Señor Aguirre: Sí, _____ dos en casa.

2. *Pablo:* ¿Qué hace los sábados por la mañana?

   Señor Aguirre: _____ los deberes de la casa.

3. *Pablo:* ¿Oye usted música?

   Señor Aguirre: _____ un poco de música cuando estoy en casa.

4. *Pablo:* ¿Sale usted mucho por las noches?

   Señor Aguirre: No, _____ sólo los fines de semana.

5. *Pablo:* ¿Ayuda usted a su mujer en casa, pone la mesa, por ejemplo?

   Señor Aguirre: Sí, casi siempre _____ la mesa.

6. *Pablo:* ¿Qué dice usted de estos cuestionarios?

   Señor Aguirre: _____ que son muy aburridos.

Drill 4

Match the verbs with their infinitives.

vienes trabajamos quiero leo
vamos hago doy recibís decís
sé tienen vemos vivimos estáis beben sois

1. decir   *decís*   9. leer   _____
2. trabajar _____ 10. ser   _____
3. hacer   _____ 11. saber _____
4. tener   _____ 12. recibir _____
5. querer   _____ 13. venir _____
6. ir   _____ 14. estar _____
7. ver   _____ 15. vivir _____
8. dar   _____ 16. beber _____

85

8.7 Hay, estar y ser
Hay, estar, *and* ser

"*Ser*" is used to express natural or inherent characteristics, definitions, colors, occupations, religion, nationality, kinship, and time.
"*Estar*" is used to express temporary conditions or states, location or position, and resultant states.
"*Hay*" is used before nouns with an indefinite article or with no article, and before numbers.

Complete the sentences with the correct form of ser, estar, **or** hay.

1. María _____ en Lima.

2. ¿ _____ un restaurante español por aquí?

3. Lorenzo _____ boliviano.

4. Susana _____ muy cansada hoy.

5. Ellos _____ muy simpáticos.

6. – ¿Qué hora _____ ? – _____ las doce.

7. Mis primos _____ resfriados.

8. _____ doscientas personas en el estadio.

9. Este coche _____ de Mariela.

10. Las tiendas _____ abiertas hoy.

11. Mario _____ comerciante.

12. Mi madre _____ jubilada.

13. Manuel _____ mi hermano.

14. El museo_____ en la Plaza Mayor.

15. Delante de la farmacia _____ una moto.

16. La moto _____ de Miguel.

86

8.8 Futuro con ir
The Near Future

To express an action that will take place in the near future, use "*ir a*" + an infinitive.

Ask the following people what they are about to do. Then put yourself in their role and give the appropriate answers. Use the near future.

1.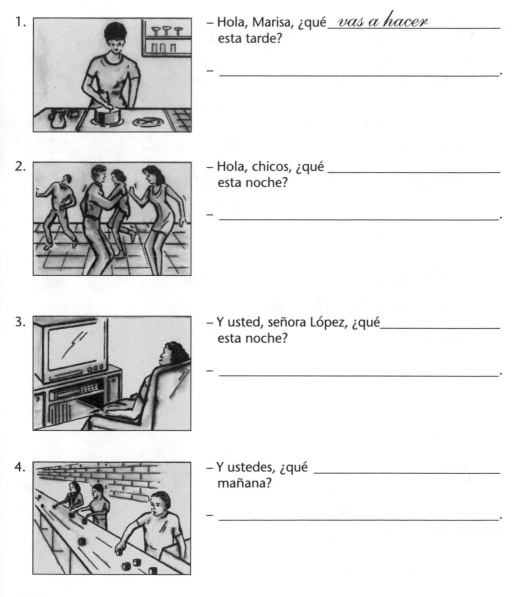
– Hola, Marisa, ¿qué *vas a hacer* _____
esta tarde?

– _____.

2.
– Hola, chicos, ¿qué _____
esta noche?

– _____.

3.
– Y usted, señora López, ¿qué_____
esta noche?

– _____.

4.
– Y ustedes, ¿qué _____
mañana?

– _____.

Gerundio con estar

The Progressive Form

The present participle is used with *estar* to express progressive action.

Formation:

Infinitive	Infinitive Stem +	Present Participle Ending
hab**lar**	habl	**ando**
com**er**	com	**iendo**
viv**ir**	viv	**iendo**

Look at the pictures. What are these people doing?
Use the verbs provided to express the actions in progress.

jugar	escribir	esquiar	correr	pasear en bicicleta	bailar
limpiar	beber	descansar	caminar	montar a caballo	pintar

1. _____

2. _____

3. _____

4. _____

5. _____

6. _____

7. _____

8. _____

9. _____

10. _____

11. _____

12. _____

8.10 Pretérito o imperfecto
Preterit or Imperfect

The <u>imperfect</u> is used for:
- customary or habitual past actions: *María se levantaba todos los días.*
- descriptions: *Hace 50 años Richardson era una ciudad pequeña.*
- two or more actions occurring at the same time: *María escribía una carta mientras José hablaba por teléfono.*

The <u>preterit</u> is used for:
- actions completed in past time: *Su padre murió a los 40 años.*
- historical events: *La Segunda Guerra Mundial estalló en 1939.*
- stating the duration of a completed action: *Ayer trabajé de 5 a 10 de la noche.*
- consecutive actions: *Ella vino, comió y se fué.*

Imperfect or preterit? Using the correct tense, fill in the blanks.

1. Antes los niños _____ en la calle, ahora es peligroso.
   jugar

2. Ayer, yo _____ en un restaurante muy bueno.
   comer

3. En 1973 Juan y Rosalía _____ a España.
   ir

4. Mientras yo _____ , mi hija _____ con la pelota.
   cocinar   jugar

5. ¿A qué hora _____ tú de la escuela, cuando _____ niña?
   salir   ser

6. Ayer nosotros _____ toda la noche.
   bailar

7. El domingo pasado, Ana _____ una carta a su marido.
   escribir

8. Hace unos años Pedro _____ mucho, ahora no.
   fumar

9. El fin de semana mis amigos y yo _____ unas cervezas.
   beber

10. Ayer nosotros _____ a casa de unos amigos, pero no
    ir

   _____ en casa.
   estar

11. La semana pasada Pedro _____ una carta de su hermana.
    recibir

8.11 Poder y saber
Poder *and* saber

Remember that *"saber"* expresses an intellectual or acquired ability.
"Poder" expresses a possibility.

Fill in the blanks with the correct form of poder *or* saber.

1. Jaime, ¿ _____ cocinar hoy?

2. ¿ _____ tú nadar? – No, no_____ nadar.

3. ¿Dónde se _____ esquiar en Suiza?

4. María _____ hablar bien inglés.

5. Mi marido _____ cocinar muy bien.

6. Los niños _____ ir a nadar esta tarde.

8.12 Los pronombres posesivos
Possessive Adjectives

Fill in the appropriate possessive pronouns.

Mi familia

1. Yo me llamo Manuela Pérez. _____ padres se llaman Jorge y Eugenia.

2. Tengo dos hermanos, una hermana que se llama Isabel y está casada.

   __ marido es Antonio, es arquitecto y trabaja en una empresa de construcción.

3. Isabel y Antonio tienen dos hijos: _____ hija mayor, Marisela,

tiene 5 años,_____ hijo menor, Roberto, tiene tres años.

4. _____ hermano se llama Ramón y está soltero, tiene una amiga.

5._____ amiga es muy simpática. 6. Yo también estoy casada,

   _____ marido es comerciante y vende coches. Tenemos dos hijas.

7. _____ hija se llama Ana y tiene 15 años,

   _____ hijo se llama Jorge y tiene 12 años.

8.13 Los pronombres interrogativos
Interrogative Words

Using these interrogative words, fill in the blanks.

¿Quién? ¿Cómo? ¿Dónde? ¿Por qué? ¿Adónde?
¿Cuántos? ¿Cuánto? ¿De dónde? ¿Cuándo? ¿Qué?

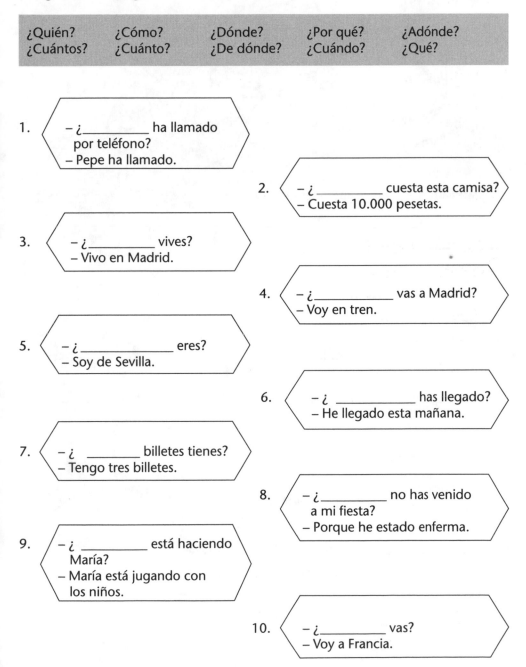

1.
– ¿_____ ha llamado
por teléfono?
– Pepe ha llamado.

2.
– ¿_____ cuesta esta camisa?
– Cuesta 10.000 pesetas.

3.
– ¿_____ vives?
– Vivo en Madrid.

4.
– ¿_____ vas a Madrid?
– Voy en tren.

5.
– ¿_____ eres?
– Soy de Sevilla.

6.
– ¿_____ has llegado?
– He llegado esta mañana.

7.
– ¿_____ billetes tienes?
– Tengo tres billetes.

8.
– ¿_____ no has venido
a mi fiesta?
– Porque he estado enferma.

9.
– ¿_____ está haciendo
María?
– María está jugando con
los niños.

10.
– ¿_____ vas?
– Voy a Francia.

8.14 Las preposiciones: a, para, por, en, de

The Prepositions a, para, por, en, de

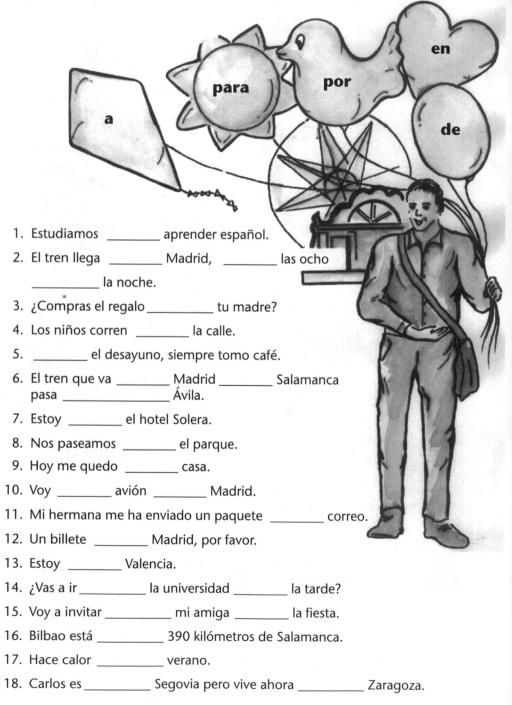

1. Estudiamos _____ aprender español.

2. El tren llega _____ Madrid, _____ las ocho _____ la noche.

3. ¿Compras el regalo _____ tu madre?

4. Los niños corren _____ la calle.

5. _____ el desayuno, siempre tomo café.

6. El tren que va _____ Madrid _____ Salamanca pasa _____ Ávila.

7. Estoy _____ el hotel Solera.

8. Nos paseamos _____ el parque.

9. Hoy me quedo _____ casa.

10. Voy _____ avión _____ Madrid.

11. Mi hermana me ha enviado un paquete _____ correo.

12. Un billete _____ Madrid, por favor.

13. Estoy _____ Valencia.

14. ¿Vas a ir _____ la universidad _____ la tarde?

15. Voy a invitar _____ mi amiga _____ la fiesta.

16. Bilbao está _____ 390 kilómetros de Salamanca.

17. Hace calor _____ verano.

18. Carlos es _____ Segovia pero vive ahora _____ Zaragoza.

8.15 Preposiciones y adverbios del lugar
Indications of Place

Match the places with the pictures.

El gato está ...
1. a la derecha de los perros.
2. delante de la casa.
3. encima de la silla.
4. a la izquierda del ratón.
5. detrás de la lana.
6. debajo de la mesa.
7. al lado del niño.
8. dentro de la caja.
9. lejos de la pelota.

¿Dónde está el gato?

a._____

b._____

c._____

d._____

e._____

f._____

g.

h.

i.

8.16 La negación
Negation

Complete the answers with the negations provided.

no ... ninguno	no ... nunca	no	no ... nada
no ... ningún	no ... nada más	no ... ninguna	
	no ... nadie		no ... ninguna

1. – ¿Hay alguien en casa?

   – No, _____ hay _____ en casa.

2. – ¿Has dicho algo?

   – No, _____ he dicho _____.

3. – ¿Han estado alguna vez en Barcelona?

   – No, _____ hemos estado_____ en Barcelona.

4. – ¿Tienes hambre?

   – No, _____ tengo hambre.

5. – ¿Tiene usted un libro interesante?

   – No, _____ tengo _____ libro interesante.

6. – ¿Hay algunos paquetes para mí?

   – No, _____ hay _____ .

7. – ¿Quedan revistas?

   – No, _____ queda_____ revista.

8. – ¿Necesitas algo más?

   – No, _____ necesito _____ .

9. – ¿Hay una parada del autobús por aquí?

   – No, _____ hay _____ parada del autobús por aquí.

8.17 Comparativo y superlativo
Comparative and Superlative

a) Compare the things listed below.

1. Océano Pacífico / Océano Atlántico - grande

   El Océano Pacífico es más grande que el Océano Atlántico .

2. Madrid / Granada - grande

   _____ .

3. Una casa / un piso - caro

   _____ .

4. Un coche / un camión - pequeño

   _____ .

5. Los padres / los abuelos - viejo

   _____ .

b) Here we test your general knowledge as well. Mark the correct answer.

1. ¿Cuál es el río más largo?
   - ❑ Misisipí
   - ❑ Nilo
   - ❑ Amazonas

2. ¿Cuál es el animal más rápido?
   - ❑ antílope
   - ❑ caballo
   - ❑ guepardo

3. ¿Cuál es el edificio más alto?
   - ❑ La torre Eiffel
   - ❑ El Empire State
   - ❑ La Torre de Madrid

4. ¿Cuál es el país más pequeño?
   - ❑ Italia
   - ❑ España
   - ❑ Andorra

Chapter 9

Juegos de palabras
Word Games

1. Have fun while learning Spanish.

In childhood you learned a great many things as you played! Put this ability to good use now, and see how easy it is to improve your knowledge of Spanish as you enjoy the games in this chapter.

2. Word games are an enjoyable way to expand your vocabulary.

If you enjoy word games, it's a good idea to do as many as possible, so that you can consolidate and expand your vocabulary.

Rompecabezas de palabras
Word Puzzle

Can you put these letters in order and make them into words?

1. _____

2. _____

3. _____

4. _____

5. _____

6. _____

7. _____

8. _____

9. _____

9.2 Mi tía de Zaragoza

My Aunt from Zaragoza

My aunt comes from Zaragoza and lives in Barcelona. Shown here are some things she likes and some things she dislikes. Try to guess why she likes some and dislikes others. Her birthplace and place of residence may give you a clue. Think about the pronunciation of Castilian Spanish!

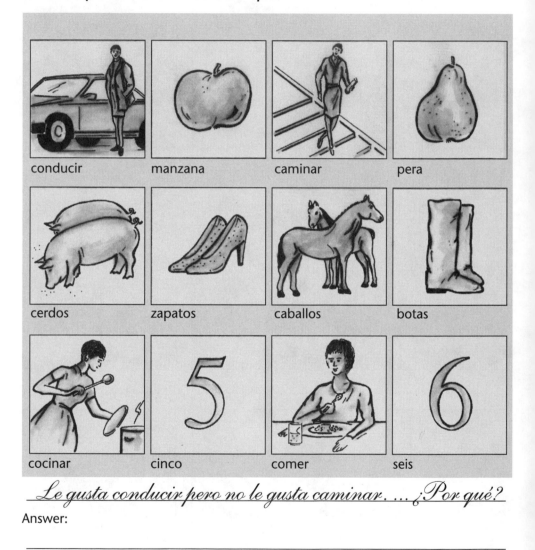

conducir	manzana	caminar	pera
cerdos	zapatos	caballos	botas
cocinar	cinco	comer	seis

Le gusta conducir pero no le gusta caminar. ... ¿Por qué?

Answer:

_____

_____

_____

Adivinanza de palabras
Riddles

Using the words provided, complete the sentences. Once you have entered the numbered letters in the right order at the bottom of the page, a message will be revealed.

moreno	niña	posible	importante	trágico	fea	joven	difícil
desesperado	Estupendo	desconocido		urgente	alto	frío	

1. Manda la carta rápido. Es __ __ __ __ __ __ __ .
    _{7 15}

2. Una chica pequeña es una __ __ __ __ .
    ₂₄

3. Lo que no se conoce: __ __ __ __ __ __ __ __ __ __ __ .
    _{3 1}

4. Es un accidente muy __ __ __ __ __ __ __ .
    _{8   9}

5. Juan viene de vacaciones. Está muy __ __ __ __ __ __ .
    _{14 16}

6. Él mide casi dos metros. Es muy __ __ __ __ .
    _{8 11}

7. ¡Es una buena idea! ¡__ __ __ __ __ __ __ __ __ !
    _{2   6   25}

8. Hace 5°C bajo cero. Hace mucho __ __ __ __ .
    ₁₉

9. ¡Eso no es __ __ __ __ __ __ __ !
    _{13   26}

10. Esa pintura es muy __ __ __ .
    ₁₂

11. Tiene sólo 13 años. Es muy __ __ __ __ __ .
    _{5 18}

12. Alimentarse bien es muy __ __ __ __ __ __ __ __ __ .
    _{22   20}

13. Está __ __ __ __ __ __ __ __ __ __ __ porque su hija no viene visitarlo.
    _{17 21   23}

14. ¡Es un ejercicio muy __ __ __ __ __ __ __ !
    _{10 4}

Message:

¡__ __ __ __ __ __ __ __ __ __ __ __ __ __ __ __ __ __ __ __ __ __ __ __ __ !
_{1 2   3 4 5 6 7 8 9 10 11   12 13 14 15 16 17 18 19   20 21 22 23 24 25 26}

Test 1

Which of the two sentences (a or b) has the same meaning as the statement given? Mark the correct answer.

1. Todos los vecinos deben haber oído eso.
   - ☐ a. Los vecinos deben oír eso.
   - ☐ b. Probablemente los vecinos han oído eso.

2. A lo mejor está en casa.
   - ☐ a. Es mejor si está en casa.
   - ☐ b. Posiblemente está en casa.

3. No puedo quedarme mucho tiempo.
   - ☐ a. No tengo que quedarme mucho tiempo.
   - ☐ b. Tengo que irme pronto.

4. No queda ninguno.
   - ☐ a. No hay más.
   - ☐ b. Hay pocos.

5. Soy siempre puntual.
   - ☐ a. Llego siempre.
   - ☐ b. Llego siempre a tiempo.

6. ¡Eso es una barbaridad!
   - ☐ a. ¡Eso es muy aburrido!
   - ☐ b. ¡Eso es terrible!

7. Todavía no he comido nada.
   - ☐ a. No he comido mucho hoy.
   - ☐ b. Hasta ahora no he comido.

8. Juan ya ha estado en Francia.
   - ☐ a. Juan estuvo una sola vez en Francia.
   - ☐ b. Juan ha estado alguna vez en Francia.

Test 2

a) Match the items in the left column with those on the right to form complete sentences.

1. Un artista
2. La secretaria
3. Un cocinero
4. Un maestro
5. Un campesino
6. Un chófer
7. Un guía
8. Una enfermera
9. Un camarero
10. Los bomberos

☐ a. prepara comidas.

☐ b. trabaja en un restaurante.

☐ c. trabaja en una escuela.

☐ d. trabaja en el campo.

☐ e. trabaja en un hospital.

☐ f. manda un fax.

☑ g. pinta cuadros.

☐ h. apagan los incendios.

☐ i. lleva a los turistas por la ciudad.

☐ j. conduce un taxi o un autobús.

b) Which nouns go with the following general concepts? Choose the right categories.

casa	autobús	fresa	falda	cama	avión
mesa	plantas	edificio	pradera	coche	leche
bosque	piso	silla	pantalones	camisa	mantequilla

1. Alimentos _____ _____ _____

2. Muebles _____ _____ _____

3. Transportes _____ _____ _____

4. Cosas que son verdes _____ _____ _____

5. Ropa _____ _____ _____

6. Viviendas _____ _____ _____

Test 3

Which word or group of words doesn't belong? Draw a circle around it.

1. peruano   español   alemán   (Austria)

2. médica   secretaria   hospital   dentista

3. padre   madre   abuela   soltero

4. moreno   rojo   rubio   alto

5. cocina   dormitorio   silla   baño

6. interesante   feliz   triste   preocupado

7. jugar al tenis   jugar al fútbol   ver la televisión   esquiar

8. pueblo   río   ciudad   ver

9. supermercado   farmacia   panadería   bar

10. arroz   traje   carne   azúcar

11. paella   tortilla   té   gazpacho

12. pescado   fresa   manzana   naranja

13. hace frío   hace sol   hay niebla   hay

14. crear   cocina   cocinar   cocinero

15. tener fiebre   tener hambre   tener frío   hace calor

16. ¡Adiós!   ¡Hola!   ¡Buenos días!   ¡Buenas tardes!

17. señor   hombre   señora   señorita

18. ciudad   cinco   cine   zapato

Test 4

What would you answer in these situations? Mark the correct answer.

1. ¿Conoces a Mercedes?
    - ☐ a. Sí, mucho gusto en conocerla.
    - ☐ b. Encantado.
    - ☐ c. Sí, es muy simpática.

2. Hola. ¿Qué tal?
    - ☐ a. Muy bien, gracias, ¿y tú?
    - ☐ b. Hasta luego.
    - ☐ c. Encantado de conocerle.

3. Me duele mucho la cabeza y tengo gripe.
    - ☐ a. No tiene importancia.
    - ☐ b. Que le vaya bien.
    - ☐ c. Lo siento, que se mejore.

4. Me llamo José Figueres, ¿y usted?
    - ☐ a. Soy ingeniero.
    - ☐ b. Me llamo Juan Pérez.
    - ☐ c. Le presento al señor Gómez.

5. ¿Cómo vais a la piscina?
    - ☐ a. Vamos en coche.
    - ☐ b. Lo siento, pero hoy no puedo.
    - ☐ c. Muchas gracias y hasta pronto.

6. ¿Puedo hablar con el señor Martínez?
    - ☐ a. Es que ahora no puedo.
    - ☐ b. Siento llamarle a esta hora.
    - ☐ c. Lo siento, ahora no está.

7. Buenos días, quisiera unos zapatos.
    - ☐ a. ¿Qué número calza?
    - ☐ b. ¿Qué talla tiene?
    - ☐ c. ¿De qué tamaño los quiere?

8. Mañana voy de vacaciones a Perú.
    - ☐ a. ¡Buen viaje!
    - ☐ b. ¡Felicidades!
    - ☐ c. ¡Qué pena!

Test 5

Choose the correct word and write it in the blank.

1. – Oye, ¿esa maleta _____ tuya? – No, no es mía.

   a. es   b. está   c. estuvo

2. Me _____ la cabeza.

   a. dolor   b. tengo   c. duele

3. La farmacia está exactamente _____ del Correo.

   a. junto   b. delante   c. frente

4. Estos trajes me parecen _____ caros.

   a. demasiado   b. bastantes   c. mucho

5. Le pedimos al _____ del hotel que nos mande un taxi.

   a. recepcionista   b. azafata   c. vendedor

6. Desde nuestra ventana vemos a Ramona. Es _____ y muy simpática.

   a. de pie   b. rubia   c. marrón

7. _____ 40 años.

   a. Soy   b. Tengo   c. Hago

8. – ¿Le queda alguna revista? – Lo siento, no me queda _____ .

   a. nada   b. ninguna   c. algún

9. ¿Tomas café _____ postre?

   a. después del   b. detrás   c. luego

10. Oiga, ¿ _____ cuesta este pescado?

    a. cuánto   b. qué   c. cómo

11. Adiós, Pepe, _____ pasado mañana.

    a. a   b. hasta   c. dentro

12. ¿Has oído las noticias _____ la radio?

    a. en   b. a   c. para

13. – Lo siento, es tarde. – No _____ .

    a. es verdad   b. importa   c. está bien

14. París es una _____ ciudad.

    a. grande   b. alta   c. gran

15. – ¿Qué hora es? – _____ las cuatro y media.

    a. Es   b. Son   c. Están

Soluciones
Answers

1.2 1. f 2.d 3.g 4.e 5.i 6.b 7.a 8.c 9.h

1.3 1. What are we doing today? 2. Juan has grown old. 3. It's very cold today. 4. Do we prepare the meal together? 5. Pack the bags, please!

1.4 1. la estación 2. los habitantes 3. la playa 4. la plaza 5. el hotel 6. el invierno 7. el palacio 8. la paella 9. la familia 10. el turista

1.5 1. de casa 2. las camas 3. una cerveza 4. al cine 5. hambre 6. un paseo 7. en casa 8. al tenis

1.6 1. interesante 2. trabaja 3. información 4. necesaria 5. camino 6. cena 7. viaje

1.7 1. triste 2. grande 3. nuevo 4. bajo 5. largo 6. limpio 7. malo 8. noche 9. correcto 10. ligero 11. viejo 12. calor

1.8 Picture 1: 1,6 Picture 2: 2,5 Picture 3: 3,7 Picture 4: 4,8

1.9 **Drill 1** 1. no 2. sí 3. no 4. no 5. sí 6. no
Drill 2 1a. español 1b. francesa 1c. alcohólicas 1d. curioso 2a. en 2b. de 2c. a 2d. (por) 2e. en 2f. a 3a. todos 3b. temprano 3c. tarde 3d. durante 3e. un 3f. últimos 4a. pueblo 4b. pueblo 4c. don Pepe 4d. la plaza 4e. don Pepe 4f. pueblo 4g. frontera

1.10 1. habitación 2. hotel 3. coche 4. tren 5. restaurante 6. traje de baño 7. gafas de sol 8. cine 9. teatro 10. tienda 11. cheque de viaje 12. pasaporte

2.1 1. manzana, carne, arroz, sopa, pescado, verdura 2. médico, mecánico, profesor, conductor, policía, campesino 3. coche, avión, autobús, barco, tren, taxi 4. silla, cama, radio, nevera, mesa, armario 5. jugar, arte, música, leer, excursión, toros

2.2 1. día 2. estrella 3. vista 4. hielo 5. calle 6. chico 7. amigo 8. madre 9. cama 10. debajo 11. antes 12. bar 13. saber 14. mesa 15. haces 16. suiza 17. vaso

2.3 1. el lunes por la mañana 2. el martes por la noche 3. el miércoles por la tarde 4. el domingo por la tarde 5. el lunes por la tarde 6. el jueves por la tarde 7. el viernes al mediodía 8. el sábado por la noche 9. el martes por la mañana 10. el jueves por la mañana

2.4 1. Invierno 2. Primavera 3. Verano 4. Otoño a. Diciembre b. Enero c. Febrero d. Marzo e. Abril f. Mayo g. Junio h. Julio i. Agosto j. Septiembre k. Octubre l. Noviembre

2.5 1. el 17 de diciembre de 1830 2. el 12 de octubre de 1492 3. el 21 de julio de 1969 4. el 6 de agosto de 1945 5. el 2 de septiembre de 1945 6. el 22 de noviembre de 1963 7. el 3 de octubre de 1990

2.6 **Drill 1** 1. mil novecientos treinta y cuatro 2. tres mil doscientos cincuenta 3. ciento cuarenta y siete 4. doscientos sesenta y dos 5. cuatro mil quinientos ochenta y cinco 6. cuatrocientos veintiuno 7. dos mil trescientos diez 8. setecientos noventa y nueve
Drill 2 1.a 2.d 3.c 4.e 5.f 6.b

2.7 1.e 2.c 3.d 4.a 5.b

2.8 **positive** 2, 3, 4, 6, 13 **negative** 1, 5, 7, 8, 14, 15, 16 **neither** 9, 10, 11, 12

2.9 1.d 2.c 3.g 4.b 5.h 6.a 7.e 8.f

2.10 1. va 2. van 3. entra 4. pasa 5. llega 6. viene 7. entra 8. pasa

3.1 **Drill 1** 1.c 2.e 3.f. 4.b 5.a 6.d **Drill 2** 1.g 2.f 3.d 4.a 5.b 6.c 7.e

3.2 **Drill 1** 1. peruana 2. España 3. suizo 4. venezolana 5. alemana 6. Ecuador 7. austríaca 8. inglesa
Drill 2 1. francés 2. italianos 3. holandés 4. españolas 5. alemán 6. argentino 7. colombiano

3.3 **Drill 1** 1. hospital 2. maestra 3. camarero 4. estudiante 5. oficina 6. ingeniero 7. azafata
Drill 2 1. cocinero 2. bombero 3. secretaria 4. peluquera 5. mecánico 6. dentista

3.4 1. Pedro 2. Rosa 3. Jorge 4. Iris 5. Gabriela 6. Ernesto 7. Miriam 8. Isabel 9. Carlos 10. Pedrito

3.5 a.3 b.5 c.2 d.1 e.4 f.6

3.6 a.3 b.1 c.5 d.2 e.4 f.8 g.6 h.7

3.7   **Drill 1** 1. el techo 2. la chimenea 3. el lavabo 4. el dormitorio 5. el baño 6. la cocina 7. la sala de estar 8. el garaje 9. la puerta 10. la ventana 11. el jardín
Drill 2 la sala: 1. el sofá 2. el sillón 3. el televisor 4. la lámpara de pie la cocina:1. el horno 2. la cocina 3. la nevera el dormitorio: 1. el armario 2. la almohada 3. la cama 4. la mesilla de noche el comedor: 1. la mesa 2. las sillas

3.8   1. escuchar música clásica, hacer punto, coser, leer novelas, hacer películas de video, tocar la guitarra 2. escuchar música pop, ver la televisión, hacer fotos, coleccionar sellos, jugar a las cartas, leer tebeos

3.9   1. hacer ciclismo 2. esquiar 3. jugar al fútbol 4. jugar al balonmano 5. nadar 6. patinar sobre hielo 7. hacer atletismo 8. jugar al golf 9. hacer la vela 10. hacer equitación 11. jugar al tenis 12. jugar al baloncesto

3.10   1. el pueblo 2. el bosque 3. la montaña 4. la colina 5. la cascada 6. la carretera 7. la ciudad 8. el puente 9. la pradera 10. el río 11. el puerto 12. el aeropuerto 13. la isla

3.11   2, 4, 5, 6, 7, 9, 10, 12, 13, 15, 16, 17, 19, 20

3.12   **Drill 1** 1. el taxi 2. el camión 3. el avión 4. el coche 5. el autobús 6. el tren 7. el barco 8. la moto 9. la bicicleta
Drill 2 1. tren 2. pie 3. barco 4. autobús 5. avión

3.13   a.1 b.3 c.5 d.4 e.6 f.2

3.14   **a)** 1. leche, arroz, vino, queso (galletas) 2. botas, zapatillas, zapatos, sandalias 3. pasteles, pan (galletas) 4. vestidos, jerseys, pantalones, faldas 5. libros 6. pescado, mariscos, gambas 7. carne, chuletas 8. manzanas, peras, uvas 9. revistas, sellos, bolígrafos, periódicos
b) A. radio-casete B. traje C. juguetes D. papel para cartas

3.15   **Entradas:** gazpacho, ensalada mixta, sopa de verduras, ensalada de lechuga, tortilla española **Plato Principal:** filete con patatas fritas, gambas a la plancha, chuletas con ensalada, pollo al ajillo, merluza a la romana, paella **Postres:** macedonia de fruta, flan, pudín, helado, fruta **Bebidas:** café, zumo de naranja, vino blanco, cerveza, agua mineral

3.16   **Drill 1** 1. manzana 2. plátanos 3. lechuga 4. fresas 5. coliflor 6. tomates 7. zanahoria 8. melón 9. uvas 10. sandía 11. limón 12. naranja 13. aceitunas 14. piña 15. patatas 16. pera
Drill 2 1. jamón 2. pollo 3. pescado 4. salchicha 5. carne 6. salchichón
Drill 3 1. queso 2. huevos 3. pan 4. leche 5. mantequilla 6. harina

3.17   1. Suiza 2. Brasil 3. Andalucía 4. Costa del Sol 5. Islas Canarias 6. París 7. Pirineos 8. La Mancha

3.18   1.b 2.d 3.g 4.i 5.a 6.h 7.e 8.f 9.c

3.19   A.1 B.4 C.3 D.2

3.20   1. Son las doce y veinte. 2. Son las seis menos diez. 3. Son las dos y media. 4. Son las nueve en punto. 5. Son las dos menos cuarto. 6. Son las seis y veinticinco. 7. Son las once menos dos. 8. Son las siete y tres. 9. Son las dos y cinco. 10. Son las nueve menos veinte. 11. Son las cinco y veintiseis. 12. Son las once y doce.

4.1   1. actualmente 2. adecuadamente 3. alegremente 4. amablemente 5. amistosamente 6. cómodamente 7. corrientemente 8. desesperadamente 9. exactamente 10. generalmente 11. lentamente 12. peligrosamente 13. propiamente 14. suficientemente 15. tradicionalmente 16. difícilmente

4.2   1. des 2. in 3. anti 4. des 5. des 6. in 7. anti 8. in 9. des 10. des 11. in 12. des 13. anti 14. des

4.3   1. difícil 2. enfermo 3. importante 4. alegre 5. posible

4.4   1. salir 2. visita 3. informar 4. reservación/reserva 5. desayunar 6. baño 7. llegar 8. ducha 9. aparcar 10. pregunta 11. parada 12. nieve 13. perdonar

4.5   **Drill 1** 1. una taza de café 2. una agencia de viajes 3. una camisa de algodón 4. un billete de avión 5. un vestido de noche 6. un carnet de conducir 7. un instrumento de música 8. un compañero de clase
Drill 2 1. individual 2. eléctrica 3. fotográfica 4. completa 5. industrial

5.1   1. ciudad, cine, zapato, dulce, azul 2. creer, cuidado, quedar, poco, clase 3. salchicha, mucho, leche, charlar, ducha 4. gente, viajar, hijo, mujer, jardín 5. domingo, ganar, gustar, agua, gato

5.2 **Third syllable from the last** tráfico, época, bolígrafo, cómodo, teléfono **Next to last syllable** gafas, bocadillo, árbol, comes, inteligente **Last syllable** nación, coger, comer, libertad, igual

5.3 José, Panamá, días, está, está, José, sábados, mercancía, plátanos, Después, mercancía, próxima

6.1 1. hablar de 2. queda 3. ha puesto 4. deja de 5. dejas 6. cuentan 7. hablar con 8. contar con 9. piensan 10. Me quedo 11. piensa en 12. se puso

6.2 1. cerrar 2. romperse 3. hacer 4. dar 5. estar 6. jugar 7. escuchar 8. ver 9. tener 10. decir 11. poner 12. ir 13. buscar 14. tomar 15. valer 16. hablar 17. pasar 18. llevar

6.3 1. tener 2. estar 3. hacer 4. ir 5. ser 6. tomar

6.4 **Drill 1** 1. verdad 2. importancia 3. pena 4. acuerdo 5. duda 6. favor 7. ganas 8. posibilidades
Drill 2 1. igual 2. mucho 3. guapa 4. bien 5. despacio 6. mucho

6.5 1. alegría 2. rica 3. feliz 4. bonita 5. guapo 6. triste 7. lástima 8. buen 9. contento 10. buena

7.1 **a)** Hello: 1, 3, 5, 6; Good-bye: 2, 4, 6, 7, 8 **b)** 1. tal 2. está 3. lunes 4. mañana 5. semana próxima 6. pronto 7. días 8. estás

7.2 **Drill 1** 1. Tomamos 2. Vamos 3. venir 4. venís 5. Vienen 6. gustaría. Accepted: 1, 3, 4 Declined: 2, 5, 6
Drill 2 1.b 2.a 3.a 4.a 5.b

7.3 1. está, Quién, Soy, momento 2. Hablo, desea, Necesito, día, El, por, bien, a, hasta 3. con, órdenes, Puedo, quién, parte, siento, tarde

7.4 1.a 2.d 3.f 4.e 5.c 6.b

7.5 **Drill 1** 1. sale 2. vuelta 3. retraso 4. sacar 5. andén 6. perdido
Drill 2 1. llega 2. billetes 3. sale 4. pasaportes 5. puerta 6. maletas 1.d 2.c 3.e 4.b 5.f 6.a

7.6 1.j 2.f 3.a 4.d 5.b 6.e 7.c 8.h 9.i 10.g

7.7 **a)** 1. desea 2. Póngame 3. Cómo 4. maduros 5. Algo 6. medio 7. todo 8. cuánto 9. Son 10. Tenga **b)** un kilo de fresas, medio kilo de zanahorias, dos kilos de naranjas, una piña

7.8 **Drill 1** f, j, a, h, k, d, b, g, i, l, e, c
Drill 2 1. cuchara 2. azúcar 3. cerveza 4. tinto

7.9 **Drill 1** 1.c 2.a. 3.b
Drill 2 1. Perdone, está 2. Hay 3. puedo 4. librería 5. enfrente

7.10 A3, B1, C4, D2

7.11 1. Deseo una habitación doble con ducha. 2. Quiero reservar una habitación para tres días. 3. Las llaves de la habitación, por favor. 4. ¿Dónde está el ascensor, por favor? 5. ¿Cuántos días desean pasar aquí? 6. ¿Tienen una habitación que da al patio? 7. Déme la cuenta, por favor. 8. Una habitación con ducha para dos personas. 9. ¿Dónde está el comedor, por favor? 10. ¿Puedo llamar por teléfono, por favor? 11. Nos quedamos desde el 18 hasta el 30. 12. ¿Hay piscina en el hotel?

7.12 1.b 2.d. 3.k 4.g 5.f 6.c 7.i 8.e 9.m 10.j 11.a 12.n 13.h 14.l

7.13 Harold; Smith, Hotel "La Palma", Calle Solana Nº 57; estadounidense; coche; gris; Ford; 1990; delante de un centro comercial en Barcelona; a las 3 de la tarde.

7.14 4

7.15 **Drill 1** 1. duele 2. tengo 3. tiene, Tome 4. gracias 5. mejore
Drill 2 a.4. b.1 c.2 d.3

7.16 1.b 2.c 3.a,b 4.b 5.c 6.c,d 7.b 8.b,e

8.1 1. un, el, los periódicos 2. un, el, los programas 3. una, la, las ciudades 4. una, la, las regiones 5. una, la, las soluciones 6. un, el, los libros 7. una, la, las casas 8. un, el, los bolsos 9. un, el, los aviones 10. una, la, las veces 11. una, la, las nacionalidades 12. una, la, las compañeras 13. un, el, los accidentes 14. un, el, los trajes

8.2 **Drill 1** 1. buen tiempo 2. unos libros interesantes 3. un coche malo 4. un gran libro 5. el jefe antipático 6. una escuela moderna 7. el señor amable 8. pocas personas 9. un viaje barato 10. mucho dinero 11. una ciudad grande 12. una escritora chilena
Drill 2 1. industrial 2. buena 3. caros 4. difícil 5. española 6. bonitas

8.3 **a)** 1. muy 2. muchos 3. mucho 4. muchos 5. muy 6. muchas 7. muy 8. mucha
b) 1. poco 2. pocas 3. poco 4. poco 5. poca 6. pocos

c) 1. Tengo mucha hambre. 2. Ud. trabaja mucho. 3. Alicia habla muy bien alemán. 4. Pedro gana poco dinero. 5. Tenemos pocas botellas en la cava.

8.4 1. personalmente 2. difícil 3. rápidamente 4. cierto 5. realmente 6. Posiblemente 7. puntualmente 8. fácil 9. rápido 10. simpático 11. fácilmente 12. barata 13. lentamente 14. naturales 15. alto 16. caro 17. bajo 18. bajo

8.5 **a)** 1. trabajo, trabaja, trabajamos, trabajáis 2. beber, bebes, bebe, bebéis, beben 3. vivir, vivo, vive, vivimos, viven **b)** 1. contesta 2. habláis 3. Bebemos 4. escribes 5. recibo 6. ayuda 7. lees 8. vendemos 9. viven 10. estudia

8.6 **Drill 1** 1. piensas 2. entiende 3. empezáis 4. Prefieres 5. quieren 6. siento 7. entendemos

Drill 2 1. cuestan 2. vuelve 3. puedes 4. duermen 5. duele 6. jugamos

Drill 3 1. tengo 2. Hago 3. Oigo 4. salgo 5. pongo 6. Digo

Drill 4 1. decís 2. trabajamos 3. hago 4. tienen 5. quiero 6. vamos 7. vemos 8. doy 9. leo 10. sois 11. sé 12. recibís 13. vienes 14. estáis 15. vivimos 16. beben

8.7 1. está 2. Hay 3. es 4. está 5. son 6. es, Son 7. están 8. Hay 9. es 10. están 11. es 12. está 13. es 14. está 15. hay 16. es

8.8 1. vas a hacer, Voy a cocinar. 2. vais a hacer, Vamos a bailar. 3. va a hacer, Voy a ver la televisión. 4. van a hacer, Vamos a trabajar.

8.9 1. Está montando a caballo. 2. Está jugando. 3. Está pintando. 4. Están bebiendo. 5. Está limpiando. 6. Están corriendo. 7. Está caminando. 8. Están bailando. 9. Está esquiando. 10. Está paseando en bicicleta. 11. Están descansando. 12. Está escribiendo.

8.10 1. jugaban 2. comí 3. fueron 4. cocinaba, jugaba 5. salías, eras 6. bailamos 7. escribió 8. fumaba 9. bebimos 10. fuimos, estaban 11. recibió

8.11 1. puedes 2. Sabes, sé 3. puede 4. sabe 5. sabe 6. pueden

8.12 1. Mis 2. Su 3. su, su 4. Mi 5. Su 6. mi 7. Nuestra, nuestro

8.13 1. Quién 2. Cuánto 3. Dónde 4. Cómo 5. De dónde 6. Cuándo 7. Cuántos 8. Por qué 9. Qué 10. Adónde

8.14 1. para 2. de, a, de 3. para 4. por 5. En 6. de, a, por 7. en 8. por 9. en 10. en, a 11. por 12. para 13. en 14. a, por 15. a, a 16. a 17. en 18. de, en

8.15 a.3 b.1 c.5 d.9 e.4 f.2 g.8 h.6 i.7

8.16 1. no ... nadie 2. no ... nada 3. no... nunca 4. no 5. no ... ningún 6. no ... ninguno 7. no ... ninguna 8. no ... nada más 9. no ... ninguna

8.17 **a)** 1. El Océano Pacífico es más grande que el Océano Atlántico. 2. Madrid es más grande que Granada. 3. Una casa es más cara que un piso. 4. Un coche es más pequeño que un camión. 5. Los padres son menos viejos que los abuelos.

b) 1. Nilo 2. guepardo 3. El Empire State 4. Andorra

9.1 1. televisor 2. cámara 3. familia 4. helado 5. teléfono 6. lámpara 7. cigarrillos 8. periódico 9. llave

9.2 Since [θ] is used in Zaragoza and Barcelona, the aunt likes all words that contain z, ce, or ci pronounced as [θ]. She dislikes words that contain the sound [k]. (For further explanation, see 5.2.)

9.3 1. urgente 2. niña 3. desconocido 4. trágico 5. moreno 6. alto 7. Estupendo 8. frío 9. posible 10. fea 11. joven 12. importante 13. desesperado 14. difícil

Message: ¡Es divertido aprender español!

Test 1 1.b 2.b 3.b 4.a 5.b 6.b 7.b 8.b

Test 2 a) 1.g 2.f 3.a 4.c 5.d 6.j 7.i 8.e 9.b 10.h

b) 1. fresa, leche, mantequilla 2. cama, mesa, silla 3. autobús, avión, coche 4. plantas, bosque, pradera 5. falda, pantalones, camisa 6. casa, edificio, piso

Test 3 1. Austria 2. hospital 3. soltero 4. rojo 5. silla 6. interesante 7. ver la televisión 8. ver 9. bar 10. traje 11. té 12. pescado 13. hay 14. crear 15. hace calor 16. ¡Adiós! 17. hombre 18. zapato

Test 4 1.c 2.a 3.c 4.b 5.a 6.c 7.a 8.a

Test 5 1.a 2.c 3.b 4.a 5.a 6.b 7.b 8.b 9.a 10.a/b 11.b 12.a 13.b 14.c 15.b

Glosario
Glossary

This glossary contains words from Chapters 1 through 9, as well as the tests, listed in alphabetical order. The words chosen for inclusion here are those that are not likely to be part of a beginner's vocabulary. It is not an exhaustive list; the common, everyday words that students of Spanish see again and again have been omitted.

The Spanish entries are in the left-hand column. In the center column are the locations where the words first occur in this book: 7.6, for example, is Chapter 7, Exercise 6. Words used in this book in different meanings are listed separately.

The gender of each noun is indicated with *m* for masculine nouns, *f* for feminine: *alquiler m, bota f.* M/f means that the masculine and feminine forms are identical: *periodista m/f.*

Feminine forms of nouns are given as follows: 1. *o, a* means that the feminine ending *a* takes the place of the masculine ending *o: abogado, a = el abogado, la abogada;* 2. *or(a)* means that *a* is attached to the masculine form: *conductor(a) = el conductor, la conductora.*

For verbs with irregular present tense forms, help is provided: *ie, ue, i,* and *zco.*

For adjectives ending in *o,* the feminine ending is indicated: *calvo, a.*

Abbreviations:

m	masculine	*mpl*	masculine plural	*Am*	Latin Americanisms
f	feminine	*fpl*	feminine plural	*s.o.*	someone

A

a lo mejor	Test 1	perhaps
a partir de	7.10	starting from
abogado, a *m,f*	2.2	lawyer
aburrido, a	2.8	boring
adecuado, a	4.1	suitable
afortunado, a	4.1	fortunate
afueras *fpl*	7.14	suburbs, outskirts
ajillo *m*	3.15	garlic
albergue *m* de juventud	7.10	youth hostel
alcohólico, a	1.9	alcoholic
alegre	1.7	merry
algodón *m*	4.5	cotton
alimentarse	9.3	to feed oneself
alimentos *mpl*	2.1	foods
almohada *f*	3.7	pillow
alojamiento *m*	7.10	lodging
alojarse	7.10	to stay at
alquilar	7.14	to rent
alquiler *m*	7.14	rent
alto, a	8.4	kind
amable	4.1	loud
amistoso, a	4.1	friendly
andén *m*	7.5	platform
anticomunista	4.2	anticommunist
antipático, a	8.2	disagreeable
aparcamiento *m*	4.4	parking place
aparcar	4.4	to park
aprobar *(ue)*	2.9	to pass (an exam)
arena *f*	1.4	sand
armario *m*	2.1	armoire
artículos *mpl* electrodomésticos	3.14	electrical appliances
asesinato *m*	2.5	murder
atardecer *m*	1.8	late afternoon
atletismo *m*	3.9	athletics
austríaco, a *m,f*	3.2	Austrian
aventura *f*	7.10	adventure
azafata *f*	3.3	stewardess

B

baile *m*	3.2	dance
bajo	8.4	softly
bajo, a	1.7	short
baloncesto *m*	3.9	basketball
balonmano *m*	3.9	handball
bebé *m*	3.4	baby
bebida *f*	1.9	beverage
bilingüe	7.16	bilingual
billete *m* de ida y vuelta	7.5	round-trip ticket
bocadillo *m* de guayaba *(Am)*	7.12	*sweet made of guava and wrapped in banana leaves*
bodega *f*	8.3	wine cellar
boleto *m (Am)*	7.12	ticket
bombero *m*	3.3	fireman
bota *f*	3.14	boot
boutique *f*	3.14	boutique

C

caer	1.4	to fall
cajero automático	3.13	ATM
calzar	7.6	to put on (shoes)
cambio *m*	3.18	exchange rate
camino *m*	1.6	way; road
campesino, a *m,f*	2.1	farmer
campo *m* de juego	7.10	playground

candidato, a *m, f*	7.16	candidate, applicant
carnaval *m*	3.17	Mardi gras
carnet *m* de conducir	1.10	driver's license
carnet *m* de identidad	1.10	ID card
carnicería *f*	3.14	butcher's shop
carrito *m* para la compra	7.6	shopping cart
carro *m (Am)*	7.12	car
casa *f* de cambio	1.10	exchange office
casa *f* vacacional	7.10	vacation house
cascada *f*	3.10	waterfall
cerdo *m*	9.2	pig
cheque *m*	3.18	check
cheque *m* de viaje	1.10	traveler's check
chimenea *f*	3.7	chimney
chistoso, a	3.5	funny
chuleta *f*	3.14	cutlet
cita *f*	7.3	appointment
cobrar el cheque	3.18	to cash the check
coche-cama *m*	7.5	sleeping car
cocina *f*	3.7	kitchen; stove
cocina *f* eléctrica	4.5	electric stove
cocina *f* equipada	7.14	fully equipped kitchen
cocinar	8.8	to cook
coleccionar	3.8	to collect
coliflor *f*	3.16	cauliflower
colina *f*	3.10	hill
comedor *m*	3.7	dining room
comerciante *m,f*	8.12	trader
cometer	2.8	to commit
cometer un error	2.8	to make an error
conductor(a) *m(f)*	2.1	driver; *(Am)* conductor
confección *f* caballeros	3.14	men's ready-to-wear
conocimiento *m*	7.16	knowledge
consigna *f*	7.5	checkroom
consultorio *m*	7.3	doctor's office
consumo *m*	5.3	consumption
contar *(ue)*	2.9	to tell
contestador *m* automático	3.13	answering machine
contrabandear	1.9	to smuggle
correcto, a	1.7	correct
Correos *mpl*	3.11	Post Office
corriente	4.1	current
coser	3.8	to sew
cruzar	1.9	to cross
cuarto *m* de estar	3.7	living room
cuenta *f*	3.13	bill
cuenta *f*	3.18	account
cuestionario *m*	8.6	questionnaire
cultivar	5.3	to cultivate; to grow
cuñado, a *m,f*	3.4	brother-in-law, sister-in-law
curso *m* de formación	7.16	continuing education, training seminar

D

damasco *m (Am)*	7.12	apricot
de repente	2.9	suddenly
deberes *mpl* de la casa	8.6	housework
decisión *f*	6.3	decision
dedicarse a	3.1	to pursue as an occupation
departamento *m*	7.16	department
desconocido, a	4.2	unknown
descubrimiento *m*	2.5	discovery
descubrir	4.2	to discover
desempleo *m*	4.2	unemployment
desesperado, a	4.1	desperate
desierto *m*	1.8	desert
desigual	4.2	unequal
desilusionado, a	3.6	disappointed
desventaja *f*	4.2	disadvantage
doler *(ue)*: me duele la muela	8.6	to hurt: my tooth hurts
dominio *m*	7.16	control
dormitorio *m*	3.7	bedroom
dulce *m* de guayaba	7.12	*sweet made from guava*

E

edificio *m*	1.8	building
empleado, a *m, f*	3.3	employee
empresa *f* constructora	7.16	construction company
empresa *f*	3.1	company
empresa *f* de construcción	3.1	construction company
en confianza	1.9	in confidence
en fin	1.9	finally
en función de	7.16	in accordance with
en monedas	3.18	in change
encantar	3.17	to delight
enfadadísimo, a	2.9	extremely angry
enseguida	2.8	at once
enterarse	2.9	to learn
escritor(a) *m(f)*	3.2	writer
esposa *f*	3.4	wife
esquiar	3.9	to ski
esquina *f*	7.9	corner
estación *f* de metro	3.11	subway station
estadio *m*	8.7	stadium
estampilla *f (Am)*	7.12	stamp
estar enfadado, a con alguien	3.6	to be angry at s.o.
estómago *m*	2.2	stomach
estrella *f*	2.2	star
examen *m*	2.9	exam
excursión *f*	2.1	excursion
experiencia *f*	7.16	experience
extender *(ie)*	3.18	to issue

F

fatal	2.8	disastrous
fax *m*	3.13	fax
fijo, a	7.16	fixed, firm

final *m*	2.5	end
formativo, a	7.16	formative
fresa *f*	3.16	strawberry
frontera *f*	1.9	border
fuente *f*	1.9	fountain
fuera de	3.17	outside
furioso, a	3.6	furious

G

gafas *fpl* de sol	1.10	sunglasses
galleta *f*	3.14	cookie
gambas *fpl*	3.14	shrimp
garganta *f*	7.15	throat
gazpacho *m*	1.4	*cold tomato soup*
gimnasia *f*	2.3	calisthenics
grado *m*	5.3	grade, class
grandes almacenes *mpl*	7.6	department store
granja *f*	5.3	farm
gris	7.13	gray
guagua *f (Am)*	7.12	bus
guardar	5.3	to keep
guardia *m*	1.9	guard
guepardo *m*	8.17	cheetah
guerra *f*	2.5	war

H

hacer alpinismo	7.10	to do mountain climbing
hacer ciclismo	3.9	to ride a bike
hacer equitación	3.9	to ride (horseback)
hacer la vela	3.9	to sail
hacer punto	3.8	to knit
hacerse mucha ilusión	2.9	to have high hopes
harina *f*	3.16	flour
hielo *m*	2.2	ice
horno *m*	3.7	oven
huevo *m*	3.16	egg

I

incapaz	4.2	incapable
incendio *m*	Test 2	fire
independiente	4.2	independent
indudable	2.8	doubtless
insoportable	2.9	unbearable
insoportable	4.2	intolerable
intolerante	4.2	intolerant

J

jersey *m*	2.2	sweater
jubilado, a	1.9	retired
jugo *m (Am)*	7.12	juice
juguete *m*	3.14	toy
juguetería *f*	3.14	toy store

L

labor *f*	5.3	work
lámpara *f* de pie	3.7	floor lamp
largo, a	1.7	long
lavadora *f*	1.4	washing machine
lechuga *f*	3.15	lettuce
legumbre *f*	5.3	legume
libertad *f*	5.2	freedom
librería *f*	3.14	book store
ligero, a	1.7	light
limpio, a	1.7	clean
llover *(ue)*	3.19	to rain
lluvia *f*	2.2	rain
lugar *m*	1.4	place

M

macedonia *f* de fruta	3.15	fruit salad
maduro, a	7.7	ripe, mature
maestro, a *m,f*	3.3	elementary school teacher
mariscos *mpl*	3.14	shellfish
medir *(i)*	9.3	to measure
melón *m*	3.16	melon
mercancía *f*	5.3	goods
merluza *f*	3.15	hake
mesilla *f* de noche	3.7	bedside table
miedo *m*	3.6	fear
molino *m* de viento	3.17	windmill
moneda *f*	3.18	coin
montar a caballo	8.9	to ride a horse
muerte *f*	2.5	death
muñeca *f*	7.6	doll

N

nadar	1.8	to swim
naturaleza *f*	7.10	nature
nevar *(ie)*	3.19	to snow
nevera *f*	2.1	refrigerator
niebla *f*	3.19	fog
nietos *mpl*	3.4	grandchildren
nieve *f*	1.4	snow
novela *f*	3.8	novel

O

objetos *mpl* caseros	2.1	household objects
odiar	3.6	to hate
oficina *f*	3.3	office
oficina *f* de Correos	3.11	Post Office
oficio *m*	2.1	occupation
ofrecer *(zco)*	7.16	to offer
ordenador *m*	3.13	computer
organizar	4.5	to organize

P

panadería *f*	3.14	bakery
panecillo *m*	7.6	roll
papa *f (Am)*	7.12	potato
papel *m* para cartas	3.14	stationery
papelería *f*	3.14	stationery store
pasajero, a *m,f*	3.3	passenger
pasear en bicicleta	8.9	to ride a bike
pastel *m*	3.14	cake
pastelería *f*	3.14	pastry shop
patinar sobre hielo	3.9	to skate
patio *m*	7.11	patio, courtyard
pediatría *f*	7.16	pediatrics

pelear	2.9	to fight
peluquero, a *m,f*	2.2	hairdresser
pera *f*	3.14	pear
perder	7.5	to miss (train, etc.)
periodista *m/f*	2.2	journalist
pesado, a	1.7	heavy
pescadería *f*	3.14	fish market
piña *f*	3.16	pineapple
plata *f (Am)*	7.12	money
plátano *m*	3.16	banana
pollera *f (Am)*	7.12	skirt
poner la mesa	8.6	to set the table
por parte de	7.16	on the side of, on the part of
posibilidad *f*	6.4	possibility
pradera *f*	3.10	meadow
preferir *(ie)*	7.8	to prefer
preocupado, a	3.6	worried
probable	2.8	probable
puerta *f*	7.5	exit

Q

quedarse	7.11	to stay
quedarse en casa	1.5	to stay at home

R

radio-casete *f , m*	3.14	radio cassette
raro, a	1.9	strange
ratón *m*	8.15	mouse
reciente	7.16	recently
regresar	1.9	to return
renovado, a	7.14	renovated
requerir	7.16	to require, need
reserva *f*	7.5	seat reservation
retirar	3.18	to withdraw
retraso *m*	7.5	delay
reunificación *f*	2.5	reunification
reunión	7.3	meeting
revisar	1.9	to check, re-examine
rey *m*	1.4	king
robado, a	7.13	stolen
robo *m*	7.13	theft

S

sacar dinero	3.13	to take out money
sacar la cuenta	3.13	to figure out the bill
sacar reserva	7.5	to make a reservation
salario *m*	7.16	salary
salchicha *f*	3.16	sausage
salchichón *m*	3.16	salami
salón-comedor *m*	7.14	living and dining room
sandalia *f*	3.14	sandal

sandía *f*	3.16	watermelon
sándwich *m (Am)*	7.12	sandwich
semáforo *m*	3.11	traffic light
sillón *m*	3.7	armchair
sitio *m*	1.4	place, spot
solución *f*	8.1	answer, solution
sonreír *(i)*	1.9	to smile
sucio, a	1.7	dirty
sueldo *m*	7.16	salary
suéter *m (Am)*	7.12	sweater
suficiente	4.1	enough

T

tebeo *m*	3.8	comic
techo *m*	3.7	roof
tener cariño a alguien	2.9	to be fond of s.o.
tenista *m/f*	3.2	tennis player
tiempo *m* libre	2.1	free time
terrible	2.9	terrible
tienda *f* de campaña	7.10	tent
tinto *m (Am)*	7.12	black coffee
título *m*	7.16	professional degree
tontería *f*	2.8	stupidity
torcer *(ue)*	7.9	to turn (right or left)
toros *mpl*	2.1	bullfight
trágico, a	2.9	tragic
traje *m* de baño	1.10	bathing suit
tratamiento *m* de textos	7.16	word processing

U

urgente	9.3	urgent

V

uva *f*	3.14	grape
vaqueros *mpl*	7.6	jeans
vaso *m*	2.2	glass
vecino, a *m,f*	Test 1	neighbor
verdura *f*	2.1	vegetables
vestido, a	3.5	dressed
viaje *m* en grupo	7.10	group travel
viento *m*	2.2	wind
vino *m* rosado	7.8	rosé (wine)
visita *f* guiada	7.10	guided tour
vista *f*	2.2	sight
vivienda *f*	7.14	dwelling

Y

yerno *m*	3.4	son-in-law

Z

zanahoria *f*	3.16	carrot
zapatilla *f*	3.14	slipper
zumo *m*	3.15	juice